THE
DISTINCTIVE HOME

THE DISTINCTIVE HOME

A Vision of Timeless Design

JEREMIAH ECK, FAIA

The Taunton Press

The Taunton Press
Inspiration for hands-on living®

The Taunton Press, Inc., 63 South Main Street, PO Box 5506, Newtown, CT 06470-5506
e-mail: tp@taunton.com

THE AMERICAN INSTITUTE
OF ARCHITECTS

The American Institute of Architects, founded in 1857, is a professional society of architects with over 70,000 members in the United States and abroad. Through its national, regional, state, and local components, the AIA works to achieve more humane built environments and higher standards of professionalism for architects through education, government advocacy, community redevelopment, and public outreach activities. AIA's website is located at aia.org.

AIA, The American Institute of Architects, and the AIA logo are registered trademarks and service marks of The American Institute of Architects.

The Distinctive Home was originally published in hardcover in 2003 by The Taunton Press, Inc.

EDITORS: Peter Chapman, Zack Gaulkin
JACKET/COVER DESIGN: Carol Singer, Susan Fazekas
INTERIOR DESIGN AND LAYOUT: Robin Weiss, Susan Fazekas
ILLUSTRATOR: Scott Bricher

Library of Congress Cataloging-in-Publication Data:
Eck, Jeremiah.
   The distinctive home : a vision of timeless design / Jeremiah Eck.
      p. cm.
   ISBN-13: 978-1-56158-528-1 hardcover
   ISBN-10: 1-56158-528-9 hardcover
   ISBN-13 978-1-56158-739-1 paperback
   ISBN-10: 1-56158-739-7 paperback
1. Architectural design. 2. Building. I. Title.

 NA27250 .E33 2003
   728'.37—dc21
                              2002151820

Printed in Singapore
10 9 8 7 6 5 4 3 2 1

For my wife, Elise, and daughter, Caroline,
who understand better than I do that no
house is truly distinctive without each other

Acknowledgments

It wasn't long after I began this book that I realized the process of writing a distinctive book was going to be as hard—and ultimately as rewarding—as designing a distinctive house. It meant that a structure and balance was necessary; it also meant I would need help from the very best people who shared all aspects of my life because, in a way, this book represents a life's work to date. Thanks are in order.

Thanks to my wife, Elise, and daughter, Caroline, who gave me more time than I deserved to work on this endeavor. They, more than anyone, knew it was time for me to stop talking and finally do something about the sad state of single-family houses in this country.

T. S. Eliot's family motto became mine: *Tace aut face* (Act or be silent).

Thanks to my two partners, Paul MacNeely and Stephen Mielke, and all of our employees over two decades who have helped us design and build distinctive houses. It's not something I could ever have done by myself.

Thanks to Peter Chapman and Zack Gaulkin, my editors, whose sense of order and infinite patience showed me that writing a book and designing a house are very much the same intellectual exercise. Thanks to Jim Childs, publisher, and the many others at The Taunton Press who believed enough in this book to start it and gave the support so necessary to finish it. A special thanks to Paula Schlosser for her distinctive book design.

Thanks, too, to the other architects who contributed to the book. I share your vision, and I hope this book will show others just how good you really are.

Finally, thanks to all my clients and homeowners, past, present, and future. Ultimately, without your faith and passion no distinctive house would ever be possible.

CONTENTS

INTRODUCTION

Americans build an extraordinary number of houses every year—more than one million and counting. The evidence is all around us, in every once-vacant lot and former cornfield or meadow, in the woods at the edges of our cities and towns. But ask almost anyone who has watched the sprouting of new houses over the last three or four decades, and you'll hear the same refrain: Why are there so few houses with character out there? Why do they have to be so bland, so boring, and so much like all the others? Our houses don't seem real, truly meaningful, or authentic in our lives anymore.

I wrote this book to prove there is an alternative. With more thoughtfulness and awareness of what is possible (even without a huge budget), we *can* make homes that are truly distinctive and timeless. As an architect who has devoted my entire working

career to designing houses, I find that the loss of distinctiveness in our houses is nothing short of tragic—especially when the process of designing and building them is uncaring and the descriptions used to explain them are so often misleading. We seem to have lost our bearing about the importance of such basics as thoughtful siting or a pleasing and balanced exterior. When that happens, it's important to step back and take a fresh look at the fundamental principles that give a house character or distinctiveness. These principles—the fundamental elements of timeless design—are not mysterious. We can all understand and apply them to our houses again. That's what this book is about.

Distinctive houses avoid the sameness, blandness, and thoughtlessness of many new houses being built today. They are situated on their plots in the best possible way, present an honest and dignified face to the world, arrange rooms to make domestic life con-

venient and comfortable, and are sensuously and spiritually satisfying inside and out.

I believe that distinctiveness lives in the subtle balance
between the site, the floor plan, the exterior elements, and the
details. Each one of those elements, in turn, is made up of details
that must be balanced just the same. The four key elements reinforce each other so that one seems to grow naturally out of the
other and engenders a sense of timelessness. To illustrate these
four major design principles, I've chosen to use houses recently

designed by a number of American and Canadian residential architects. Architects don't always design the best houses, and some very good houses have been designed without an architect, but the houses shown here clearly illustrate how a balance between these elements can be achieved. Those who care deeply about their homes will find the houses especially appealing. Like an iconic New England farmhouse or a California bungalow, these are houses most of us would want to live in.

In the end, the concept of the book is simple: Better understanding of houses leads to better houses. By the time you've finished this book, you'll be able to look at a house and say not only that you like it but also *why* you like it and how you can apply its lessons in the design of your own home.

This search for timelessness is something I've experienced personally. My wife and I spent many months looking for an older house to renovate outside of Boston. The neighborhood we finally chose is filled with a mix of older and newer houses—and almost without exception, the older homes have more character, more grace, and more livability. The exterior shapes and interior spaces of the house we settled on were better proportioned and more elegant than those of newer houses. (The before [right] and after [left] versions of the house are shown in the photos above.)

Needless to say, this realization was a little disheartening for a residential architect. Why were there so few new houses with the same appeal? It was that experience that finally convinced me to write this book. For years, I had designed homes for other people and had preached my concerns about the poor quality of most houses being built, but it wasn't until I faced the cold reality of the current housing market that I realized how dire the situation had become. I know we can do better. We have done it before, and we can do it again. My hope is that the following pages will inform and support all of you who still believe that distinctive, timeless houses of lasting character are important and possible.

What makes a house distinctive?

A few years ago I designed a vacation home on a small island off the coast of Rhode Island. At just 1,200 sq. ft., it is a compact house, with an outward appearance that most people, at first glance, might describe as plain. The house (shown on the facing page) is boxy, with a steep gabled roof and cedar siding, like a New England barn. But on closer inspection, the visitor notices that the house isn't quite so straightlaced. The windows are placed asymmetrically, punctuating the rigid facade and suggesting an intriguing interior behind the wall. On the private side, facing the ocean, the walls open with windows almost as expansive as the sweeping views of the Atlantic. This is no New England farmhouse, and yet it seems to respond just as directly to its environment. The design is as practical as it is simple; it welcomes the cooling southwest summer breezes while shielding the house from the winter wind out of the north.

There are many ways a house can belong to its site. By nestling this house into the side of a slope rather than placing it on top, house and land seem to fit together naturally. There is another benefit, too: Each floor has a slightly different view.

A closer look at the house reveals its New England roots. Simple, barnlike shapes are complemented by an assortment of siding materials, trim, and window arrangements that give the house a distinctive quality.

Most people would agree that this house "belongs." As Frank Lloyd Wright might say, it sits *of* the hill not *on* it. All the pieces—from the way the house faces the ocean to the arrangement of rooms and windows—create an integrated whole. The result is that the appearance, the functionality, and the details will be appreciated just as much in 50 years as they are today by the current owners.

This sense of distinctiveness and time-lessness isn't something that happened by accident. It was a deliberate effort from the beginning of the design process.

Change the shape of the house or the position of the windows—or even their colors—and you'll see that these elements are not arbitrary. The floor plan emerged from how and where the house was situated on the property; the exterior reflects the arrangement of rooms on the inside; and the detailing, both inside and out, follows a simple logic—to make this home relate to its coastal New England environment. Imagine the house taller or wider, with different siding materials, rearranged windows, or sitting farther up the hill, and you begin to see that the balance becomes upset. I'm not claiming that this is the *only* house that would work on this site; rather, I'm suggesting that all the design elements of this house work together to produce something with lasting comfort and appeal.

The Essentials of Timeless Design

Sure, it's easy to make a house look distinctive when it sits on an island in the Atlantic, you might say. But you don't need an ocean in your backyard or an unlimited budget (these owners didn't have one) to enjoy a home that has lasting character. It's possible to create a distinctive house *anywhere*, whether you're on the seacoast or in a subdivision, and you can do it without spending a fortune. How is this possible? There is no magic formula, but my experi-

The placement of windows in any distinctive house is the result of both exterior and interior considerations. The row of south- and west-facing windows, along with a light well above that penetrates through the ceiling, gathers plenty of sun for the interior.

ence designing houses has led me to conclude that there are four essential features of every house that can have a lasting impact:

- How it occupies its site.

- How the floor plan maximizes efficiency and comfort for today's living.

- How the exterior is balanced and blends naturally with the site (or neighborhood).

Even a small house on a run-of-the-mill site can have a distinctive look. The unique rooflines, generous windows, and board-and-batten siding elevate this house above the ordinary.

A distinctive house is all about relationships. Here the exterior details—exposed framing, porch brackets, windows, and siding materials—relate to each other. Although the house borrows elements common to California bungalows, its style is all its own.

It's possible to create a distinctive house anywhere, whether you're on the seacoast or in a subdivision, and you can do it without spending a fortune.

☞ How selected exterior and interior details (such as trim, stair railings, mantels, and built-ins) transmit an enduring sense of quality, care, and thought.

These four elements are not the *only* important considerations when designing and building a house, but I believe that they are the *most* important. They work together and build on each other. The geography of a house lot helps determine the orientation of the home, which has an impact on the arrangement of rooms, or the floor plan. The floor plan, in turn, has much to do with how a home looks from the outside—the shape of the house and roofline; the placement and size of windows; and the layout of dormers, porches, and decks. Exterior and interior details complete and reinforce the overall effect.

A distinctive house—one that has a timeless repose, one that sits of the hill and not on it—strikes a subtle balance between site, floor plan, exterior elements, and details. This is the heart of the next four chapters. Spending a little extra time, thought, and effort in these four areas (and perhaps sacrificing other features) can turn a typical home on a seemingly mundane lot into something unique. The goal is not just to elicit the response "This house has character" but to create a house that complements its surroundings in a way that suggests it *belongs,* today and into the future.

BUILDING BETTER HOUSES

Building better houses sounds simple enough. After all, who wouldn't want their home to be timeless and distinctive, especially if the cost is reasonable? Unfortunately, not many, if you judge by the thousands of sprawling subdivisions around the country and the countless house plans available from lumberyards, general contractors, and over the Internet. If you're in the market for a home (as I was, not long before I started writing this book), you might begin to wonder if perhaps a law had been passed banning character in new houses. But it's not because people aren't looking for these qualities. We are. Many of us have grown up in or around homes whose proportions made sense, whose details looked and felt right. It does require extra effort, and sometimes tough choices, to create something distinctive; unfortunately, it's a lot easier to settle for what's available.

What's available isn't always pretty. Take a drive into the outskirts of any established town or suburb in America, and eventually you'll come across a subdivision brimming with new homes. You'll notice how, in most cases, they face the road like soldiers in formation, their garages competing with the house for your attention. Their details are often the same or similar—rooflines, window trim, decks, and porches. You can bet that each home, inside and out, is one in a series of variations on a theme: the two-story colonial, the raised ranch, the Tudor, or the contemporary. These are anonymous production houses, probably built from stock plans designed to appeal to the average consumer. Most of the more than one million homes built in America each year fit into this category.

The loss of valuable open space has been an unfortunate side effect of our rapid development, which is spilling (and sprawling) houses into our suburban and rural countryside. A million or more houses are built in the United States every year, and farms are one casualty.

WHAT'S MORE IMPORTANT: COMFORT OR PLEASURE?

A distinctive house provides comfort, which isn't the same thing as pleasure. Comfort describes an abiding sense of enjoyment, warmth, contentment, and, for some, a spiritual sense of well-being. Pleasure suggests entertainment, stimulation, and convenience.

Many production houses provide entertaining appliances, such as Jacuzzis, or rooms aimed at specific types of pleasures—for example, watching television, playing music, or dining. To me, one of the goals of a house should be not just to provide pleasure but to achieve a higher level of all-encompassing satisfaction. Well-proportioned spaces, good light, and small but thoughtful details can help push a home beyond mere pleasure.

Pleasure is about entertainment, whereas comfort is all about enjoyment and warmth, which only a well-designed space or detail can give you.

Houses in subdivisions often seem similar because they tend to face the road like soldiers in formation rather than taking advantage of the unique qualities of each site. All too often such houses have an anonymous quality that makes them seem as if they could have been built anywhere.

IT'S NOT ALL ABOUT SIZE

*E*ach *year more than one million single-family homes are built in the United States. More than half the single-family* homes in this country were built since 1970. Houses are getting larger, too. In 1950, the average American house was 983 sq. ft. By 1970, it had grown to 1,500 and, by 1999, it was 2,225—more than twice as big as an average home built four decades earlier. And 2,225 sq. ft. is the average; it's not unusual today to find new homes that are 4,000, 6,000, or 8,000 sq. ft.—and larger. But when you draw a floor plan on paper, 2,225 sq. ft. is not all that large if it contains a generous entry, a living, dining, and kitchen area, a master bedroom suite and two other bedrooms, and a family room or a screened porch.

While it's been fashionable lately to criticize big houses as bloated and ugly, I don't think size is the problem. Creating a house appropriate to the environment and using space thoughtfully and purposefully can happen on any scale. There are plenty of examples of large houses that don't seem too large, that feel just right. By the same token, a small house is not for everyone. I lived in one for 15 years, so I speak from experience when I say some extra room here and there is not always such a bad idea. It's not about size; it's about design.

Big houses don't have to be ugly. Here, the stone base, chimney, and natural colors of the roof and siding seem to grow out of the surrounding landscape, resulting in a harmonious design that doesn't overwhelm the site.

Production houses fulfill the needs for affordable shelter for our growing population, and that's a good thing. Homeownership in America is at an all-time high (65% of Americans now own their homes), and one of the reasons is that homes are available, in some sense, prepackaged. And there is no shortage of options. Along with the Internet has come an explosion in the number of house plans available to the consumer, and lumberyards proffer plan books the size of telephone directories. Some of these houses are well designed, but the reality is that the process of "delivering" them—while expedient (and profitable) for builders, brokers, and bankers—often leaves out the interests of the buyer and eventual homeowner. (In lots of cases, the buyer may get to select the kitchen and bathroom cabinetry, flooring, and trim colors but not much else.) The result, I've found, is a sense of emotional distance from our most important environment.

New houses don't have to be built this way. By carefully considering the four key elements of a house—siting, floor plan, exterior elements, and details—consumers, builders, and even architects may discover options for creating a distinctive home, one that transcends cookie-cutter styles and arbitrary conventions. This approach is possible no matter what your budget, but there will be trade-offs. Custom windows to capture a distant view may come at the expense of a master bathroom with a Jacuzzi; a hand-crafted front door may be possible only by eliminating the stainless-steel refrigerator. But which will do more to give the house a lasting sense of quality and comfort? So before you order a set of plans from a magazine, call a builder, or hire an architect, keep in mind the features you believe are essential, because they will go a long way toward helping you create a distinctive house of lasting character.

Site: Marrying a House to the Land

Not surprisingly, placing a house on a parcel of land is perhaps the most difficult task—and the most critical—when designing and building a home. Plan it right, and you are well on your way to creating a home that will comfort and nurture generations. Do it arbitrarily, and you're stuck with it, good or bad. Siting is difficult because so many factors come into play. Drainage and zoning are important, but so are climate, views, and sunlight as well as the surrounding topography and architecture. The path of the sun, the need for privacy from the street and driveway, the comforts of a view into a patch of woods or a distant clearing—these are things that can elevate a home to something more than merely a shelter, at little or no extra cost. Yet too often these considerations are given little thought by builders or developers.

Uniformity is sometimes unavoidable—and even desirable. Lots on city streets don't lend themselves to many siting options,

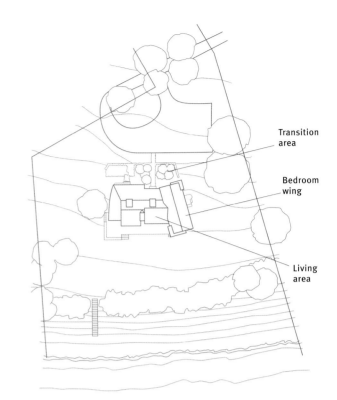

Transition area

Bedroom wing

Living area

Siting a house is a process of pushing and pulling until all the pieces fit. A slight angling of the bedroom wing opens up the view, provides sun to the living area, and accommodates the sweep of the slightly sloping site to the water. A low stone wall creates a court, which serves as a transition between the drive and the main entry.

Good siting means balancing many factors, including views, sun, topography, and greenery. The low wraparound porch that flows into an open deck and down to the ground creates a natural intimacy between the site and the house and opens up areas for outdoor activities.

Big features—rooflines, chimneys, and colors—mark a home's first impression and therefore are important to consider. The low Connecticut hills in the distance are a perfect backdrop for the steep, striped roof, massive chimney, and reddish tones of this house.

Good siting means that a house works on many levels: at a distance, up close, and from within.

and even small suburban lots seem to offer little in the way of unique siting. In these cases, the challenge becomes matching the home to the site to maximize what it *does* offer. If it's impossible to orient a house to capture the sun from the south, can you install larger windows on the south face to allow the sun to penetrate deeper into the interior rooms? What about making the house narrower so sunlight can reach into every room? What you can't control in siting you may be able to manipulate in other ways—repositioning rooms or adding skylights and dormers. The goal is to join house and land in a thoughtful, even intimate, way.

Good siting means that a house works on many levels: at a distance, up close, and from within. It means creating privacy where it is needed, positioning entryways, driveways, and garages with care and not by convention. It means taking advantage of good views, screening unwanted views, and optimizing natural light. Some of my favorite houses are those that occupy their surroundings as if they had grown out of them. Ultimately, good siting means creating comfort for the people who will be living there. For some people, this means an airy, well-lit kitchen with a view of the yard. For others, it means a master bedroom with a private view of the woods or pond. Rotating a house away from the road may open up possibilities. Placing a garage to enclose a backyard can block an adjacent house (or an adjacent lot where someday there may be a house). In some cases, a lot calls out for more separate structures

Even from a distance, a house needs to fit with the site—as if it had grown out of the land. The stone and trees in the foreground are reflected in the shapes and color of the house materials, especially the low stone wall and chimney.

(house, barn, and garage). On other lots, one structure is all that will fit.

A poorly designed house sometimes can be "good enough" for its occupants if it takes advantage of the site, whether natural or man made. On the other hand, a well-designed house can never make up for arbitrary or illogical siting. That's how important siting is. Certainly, well-designed houses would help redeem some of the repugnant visual effects of sprawl—the uncontrolled, pervasive, and monotonous construction spreading into our countryside. Better siting would also help. Imagine a development with each house positioned uniquely on its lot instead of in a row with its neighbors. In this book, I offer some alternatives.

The relationship between a house and its site is just as important close up as it is from a distance. By placing it on a stone base, the designer tied this house to its immediate surroundings.

The connection to the environment extends to the indoors as well. The stone fireplace surround is mirrored in the low outside walls, and the color of the wood floor, ceiling, and window trim is the perfect complement to the surrounding trees.

Floor Plan: Expressing the Way You Live

Siting is critical, but what good is a dramatic view if the window onto that view happens to be in a cramped, uninviting room? Along with siting, the arrangement of rooms—the floor plan—is a critical element of a house and another instance in which many unique opportunities are squandered. The two go hand in hand: A good floor plan follows from a good site plan, but that's just the beginning. A floor plan that fails to meet the basic needs of daily living undermines the success of any house design. Unfortunately, most floor plans these days are prepackaged to meet conventional expectations. A living room off the front hall is considered standard, and that's just what you will find in mass-market houses, even if no one actually uses that room (see the drawing below).

Again, there's a better way. Rather than shoe-horn people into rooms they don't need, it's worthwhile to take a step back and look at how most people live and then craft a floor plan to meet those needs. Rather than thinking of a floor plan as a series of rooms—kitchen, living room, and dining room—it's sometimes helpful to think about the *nature* of the space. Is it public or private? Formal or informal (see the drawing on the facing page)?

This is a worthwhile exercise but not always an easy one. I used to teach a course on designing houses, and I would tell my students that anyone who could create a floor plan without using any standard room descriptions such as a living room or kitchen would get an automatic A. No one ever could, probably because

Thoughtful consideration of actual, daily use of rooms in a floor plan can result in more dramatic spaces. This tall room was designed to accommodate a greater feeling of spaciousness on public, informal living occasions, but the connecting lower space also provides a more intimate feeling on rarer formal dining occasions.

A STOCK PLAN

Stock plans come in every imaginable style and are meant for a mass market eager to cut building expenses. But, by their very nature, stock plans can't take into account the unique opportunities a site may offer.

Patio

Master bedroom

Dining

Kitchen

Bed-room

Bed-room

Living room

Garage

A PLAN FOR THE WAY WE LIVE

Contemporary living requires a contemporary plan, one that allows for a free-flowing informality among spaces and new functions, such as entertaining guests while simultaneously preparing meals. The relationships between public and private, formal and informal are also different from those of the past.

Dining (informal, private)

Dining (formal, public)

Porch (informal, public or private)

Entry (private)

Garage (private)

Living hall (formal or informal, public)

Entry (public)

Rooms tailored to daily life sometimes need a new name. This large, screened space connects independent living areas for adults, children, and guests. It's a new kind of outdoor living room with sitting areas, a fireplace, and stairs to upper floors. It's not a typical screened porch and deserves a new name, such as "summer living porch."

these ideas are embedded in us from childhood. But if we can free ourselves from convention, we can look at a living room either as public place for visitors or a cozy hideaway for the family. It might be a formal room designed specifically for entertaining and displaying art or an informal space for reading and watching television. Asking yourself these questions can help you create a floor plan that really works, where the private, informal rooms are near bedrooms and the public areas are near the front door. It might

New Rooms Deserve New Names

Throughout this book I refer to rooms in the conventional way, such as dining room, bedroom, and family room. But I urge you to think of other, more descriptive names that have significance in your own daily life and routine. I use the term "living hall" to describe a room that lies somewhere between a formal living room (the room our parents never let us use) and an informal hall or gathering place that can be used by anyone, at any time.

For me, a living hall seems to fulfill the need for a room near the kitchen where visitors and family members can get together informally, during the preparation of a meal. This isn't just a semantic exercise—very often, by formulating a new name to reflect the specific function of a room, you can avoid the traps of conventional assumptions, which helps open up new design possibilities.

A combination living room, dining room, and kitchen requires a new name other than eat-in kitchen. I call it a "living hall," because it suggests an informal gathering area for a number of functions, but other names might work just as well. Renaming rooms by their function or relationship to other rooms frees the imagination and opens up new opportunities.

Breaking from conventions can open up all sorts of opportunities. Here, the architect split up a two-car garage into two single garages, creating an interesting passage into a courtyard. The combination of the court and farmhouse-like shapes (and colors) gives this complex a barnyard quality in keeping with its rural setting.

even make you realize that you don't need a traditional living room at all.

This is just one example of designing a plan for the way we really live. There are other ways to think about plans. Can you get what you need on a single floor? Or will you need a two-story (or more) plan? You may decide that some functions should be completely separate from others, resulting in multiple stairways or even a "compound plan" of more than one structure. Or you may put equal weight on your needs for inside and outdoor space, which may result in a courtyard or expansive deck with more than one entry. A good plan is one that is tailored to your needs and to the site.

A floor plan that fails to meet the basic needs of daily living undermines the success of any house design.

RETHINKING THE PLAN

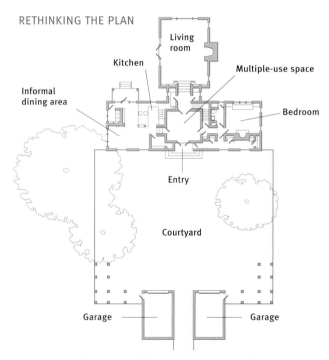

Splitting the plan in the middle **created a new multiple-use space that can act as an entry point, stair hall, library, and even formal dining area (photo at left). It also acts as a transitional space between the informal dining/kitchen area, living space, and bedroom wing of the house (floor plan above).

Traditionally, houses were built to suit the local climate. Southern houses of the nineteenth century, for example, had lots of windows for ventilation and wide overhangs that shaded the porches.

The strong character of the eighteenth-century center-entrance Colonial house or "Georgian" was derived from its direct response to climate and functional needs.

The Public Face: Balancing Function and Beauty

The arrangement of exterior walls, windows, doors, and roofline—what architects call *elevations*—follows directly from siting and floor plan. In fact, a house often looks right when it closely relates both to the outdoor environment and to the rooms within. This can be tricky, because people tend to identify houses by the way they look from the outside, and there is always a lot of pressure to adhere to some exterior styles. A rectangular, one-story house with a steeply pitched roof gabled on both ends is a Cape. Add a story, and you've got a Colonial. Make it a split-level with a hipped roof, and it's a raised ranch. Even details such as siding material, window trim, shutters, porches, and rooflines are used to classify homes into loosely identified categories such as Queen Anne, French provincial, and Shingle Style.

But just as stock floor plans often fall short of our day-to-day needs, houses built to mimic a historic style seldom make a lasting imprint on us, probably because these days they have so little to do with what's going on inside or outside the house. There's nothing wrong with borrowing features or elements from a Victorian townhouse or an Arts and Crafts bungalow, but a home's exterior works best when it also follows naturally from thoughtful siting and a sensible, workable floor plan. If you start with the idea of integrating site, floor plan, and exterior, you can discover your own vision of house. Will it have a particular style? Perhaps, but that is less important than making the fundamental decisions first. In other words, don't start with a style—end with one.

Consider the island house I mentioned earlier in this chapter. Its exterior clearly borrows elements from regional architecture, and why not? The combination of shingle and vertical siding, the steeply pitched roof, and even the square windows hearken back to the classic New England farmhouse (see the top photo on p. 22). But notice, too, that the site and floor plan have dictated other important elements—the private, sheltered north-facing wall; the wide open walls facing south and west toward the ocean; the arrangement of windows to capture views and light yet maintain privacy. What style is this? I'm not sure, but I *am* sure that the result is pleasing to the eye.

Now you might say that a home in the Cape Cod style would have been fitting for this location and perhaps even timeless, but staying true to the Cape style (or any style) would have led to major compromises, inside and out. Rather than let the style rule, the site and floor plan set the stage. I'm not suggesting that a floor plan or a view should dictate a home's exterior look. That would be a mistake—either the floor plan would make no sense or the exterior would look haphazard, a jumble of shapes. What I am suggesting is that we look at a houses as an integrated whole, where site, floor plan, *and* exterior are considered simultaneously. It's a delicate balance, but the results are worth the extra effort,

A house looks right when it closely relates both to the outdoor environment and to the rooms within.

Regional climate played a large part in determining the style of early New England houses.

The simple form and steep roof recall a New England farmhouse or barn; but the arrangement and size of the windows (strategically placed to capture sunlight and ocean views) give this house its own distinctive style while remaining true to a regional vernacular.

because a well-designed house will hold its appeal for generations, no matter what the style.

Beyond style, there are many questions to consider in choosing the exterior details of a house. Should the house look big or small, squat or tall? If the lot is on a hill, how do you prevent the house from towering over its neighbors or appearing to slide down the slope?

Should the house be a simple square or rectangle, or would it make sense to break out of the box by stretching the house into discrete sections, at different angles to each other?

Exterior detailing can make all the difference. Wide clapboards at the base and shingles at the midsection of this (mainly) one-story house lend a unique quality that not only anchors it to the landscape but also sets it apart from the typical ranch style.

Is the roofline clean and stark, or punctuated with hips and valleys or dormers, cupolas, and skylights? What about other details, such as siding, soffits, windows, porches, chimneys, and entry doors? Again, these are questions that can't fully be resolved without taking into account the vagaries of the site and the necessities of the floor plan. Only then is it really possible to create a house that sits *of* the hill and not *on* it.

Don't start with a style— end with one.

Because of the neighborhood or landscape, some houses actually benefit from appearing larger than they really are. This 4,500-sq.-ft. house sits in a neighborhood of much larger and older houses. It seems bigger because of the combination of roof types and windows and the way the garage and study are pulled away from the main body of the house.

Each side, or elevation, of a house can have its own personality, depending on the view, the need for sunlight, or for access to the outdoors as well as on more subtle considerations, such as privacy or degree of formality. The front and back of this house share the same architectural vocabulary, but the more formal rear, shown here, stands apart from the more informal entry side shown above.

Clustering three wood columns with organically detailed forged metal straps gives this exterior detail the impression of supporting trees, in perfect harmony with the Adirondack camp–like qualities of the rest of the house and the site.

The feel of a house can be uplifting or uninspiring on the basis of its details alone.

Details: The Intimate Realm

So we've figured out the best way to situate the house on its site, we've assembled a floor plan that seems to solve the needs of its occupants, and the exterior elements are falling into place. The house is starting to develop its own identity, at least on paper. What next? The last of the four elements that can help you create a distinctive home are the exterior and interior details, those parts of our homes that we live with most intimately—such as a custom-built front door, a stone fireplace, special moldings, exterior brackets, and cozy built-ins. What detail should get this added layer of attention and craftsmanship? You decide. But if a home can boast just one detail that rises above the standard, it will be noticeable, and its effect will be far-reaching, suggesting that time and care have gone into the rest of the house as well.

I've always believed that there are a few critical details, like fireplaces, that mean the most to us. I try to include at least one of these special details in every house I design. This notion also applies to older houses. If you do only one thing to improve your current house, you should lovingly work on a detail like this and make sure it expresses the artistic quality you seek in the house. The feel of a house can be uplifting or uninspiring on the basis of its details alone. More than any other element of a house, they express the aspirations and values of owners, because they exist privately and (sometimes) in unexpected places.

A fieldstone fireplace or custom-made built-ins are especially satisfying when they relate to other features of the house. Playing off a window pattern in interior trim is one way to relate two elements quite literally; having cabinetry custom milled from a tree

Finely coursed chimney-breast stone, large hearth stones, wood cabinetry and mantel, and wood flooring and ceiling not only are rich details in themselves but also relate to the natural qualities of the site.

Transparency between indoors and outdoors was clearly the goal here, achieved by running open shelving in front of the kitchen window—a perfect place for glasses. The openness is consistent with the light, airy quality of this California house.

on the property is perhaps more metaphorical but equally powerful. The opportunities to bring all the design elements together in a detail are not always obvious, but it's worth looking for them. In some cases it may be as simple as finding a place to use a natural material—a slate counter, copper gutters, wrought-iron door latches, or fir window trim. It may also take the form of a superior level of craftsmanship—such as that custom front door.

Handcraftsmanship and premium materials are expensive, and it's not realistic to think that most people can afford a fancy fireplace or a custom-made front door. But when you weigh the impact of a distinctive detail against, say, a three-car garage or an in-ground pool, which will provide more comfort over the long haul? Which will age more gracefully? Which will inspire daily enjoyment or quiet contemplation? I can't answer those questions for you. All I can do is suggest that there are choices.

Distinctiveness lives in the balance between the site, the floor plan, the exterior elements, and the details. Each one of those elements, in turn, is made up of details that must be balanced just the same. In a timeless house, the four key elements reinforce each other so that one seems to grow naturally out of the other. The next four chapters will show you just how to make this happen.

Distinctiveness lives in the balance between the site, the floor plan, the exterior elements, and the details.

A few thoughtful details can cement the marriage between house and site. At left, a blend of clear and translucent glass in the entry door, combined with a vine-covered trellis, blurs the distinction between inside and out and offers a smooth transition from one environment to the other. Above, the oversize windows in the living area of a waterside home play a similar role.

2

Marrying a house to the land

Early in my career, I was invited to help in the siting of a house along a creek in Onancock, Virginia. The owners were eager to build a new house on the property, one that would replace an ancient, decrepit farmhouse that (with the owners' permission) the local fire department had burned down for practice, leaving only a stone foundation.

The owners came with me on the site visit because they wanted to be involved in siting the new house, and I invited a landscape architect to accompany us. The property was low and marshy, so we built a platform out of plywood and 2x4s that we dragged around to get a better sense of the views from the first floor, which would have to be about 9 ft. off the marsh (see the photos on p. 30). We spent all day moving our viewing platform around, taking in the light, the scenery, and the grounds below at various positions on the property. After many hours—just as the sun was setting—we finally found a spot where everything seemed to come together. It was the highest point of land on the marsh,

Views, sun, and subtle changes in topography played big roles in siting this house on a marshy peninsula in Virginia. Before settling on a site for the foundation, the landscape architect, the owners, and the architect walked the land with a 9-ft. platform to determine the views from the first floor, which had to be raised high off the marsh.

One of the key goals in siting a house is to capture as much daylight as possible while providing shelter from bad weather. The covered porches and screened porch take advantage of the variety of weather in this coastal Virginia location. Raising the house on piers not only protects against flooding but keeps insects away from open outdoor areas.

the views were great, and the sunlight was perfect. And to our amazement, we were sitting almost dead center over the old stone foundation!

This was a humbling experience for a budding architect, but it reinforced a truth about siting that I carry with me to this day: Distinctive siting is something that we are all capable of. Even the farmer who built that original house knew something about it and got it right. Whether he was inspired by the same qualities of the property that we were is impossible to know. But he probably was.

Belonging to the Site

Siting a house is the biggest challenge in design. It poses the biggest risks, and, ultimately, it provides the most lasting satisfaction for the people who will live in the house. It's where everything begins and all options remain open. Some sites pose contradictory challenges and force maddening compromises. The best views may be to the north but the best sunlight comes from the south, or the site might be steep just where you think the front door should be. The distinctive house takes full advantage of a perfect lot just as it turns the negatives of a challenging site into something special. The goal is to tailor a home to its site in an intimate and thoughtful way so that it appears to—and actually does—*belong*.

Thoughtful siting takes time. It means getting intimate with the land, walking its boundaries, peering into its foliage, and visiting it at different times of day or in different seasons, if possible. The stakes are high. Get it right—like the farmer—and everything falls into place. Place a house haphazardly, without taking into account the unique (and distinctive) qualities of its surroundings, and there's little you can do to correct for it later. So it's well worth your while to pour time and energy into this first stage of the building process.

Not everyone will be able to point to a specific feature of the well-sited house—the way it accommodates a slope or how the floor plan takes advantage of the sunlight. In fact, the more a house blends with the landscape the more invisible its siting

The distinctive house takes full advantage of a perfect lot just as it turns the negatives of a challenging site into something special.

Exterior details help marry a house to its environment. The simple low-hipped roof of this coastal home simultaneously reflects and defers to the low-lying, rocky shoreline, which is echoed in the low terrace wall and chimney.

> *The more a house blends with the landscape the more invisible its siting becomes.*

becomes. But most people will notice something special and distinctive. Take a look at a house you like in your own neighborhood and you'll probably find this intimacy. It will be hard to see the land and the house separately. It's a marriage, and it's important whether a house hugs a desolate shoreline or sits in the middle of a teeming neighborhood.

There are many factors to consider when siting a house. Every site has its own topography, climate, sun, and views that need to be reckoned with and prioritized. There are the complexities of soil and ledge, drainage, vegetation, zoning regulations, and environmental standards to take into account. Man-made factors, such as neighboring buildings or old stonewalls, will play a role in house placement. All these decisions make siting a house a juggling act. Just keep in mind the simple lesson I learned from that long-gone farmer: Before you even think about the house, take a good look at the land on which it will stand.

Getting Started: The View from Above

Siting a house—the process of laying out a structure's footprint on the land—often comes down to mere feet and sometimes even inches, but it begins with much greater distances. If you're looking for land, you'll probably drive by a few lots first or perhaps you'll see some plot plans in a Realtor's office. Before you start looking for where the front door might be, take a step back. Think about the site in the context of the broader landscape. Where are the roads, other houses, nearby open spaces, and heavily trafficked thoroughfares? What's just over the hill or behind the trees? Where will the sun rise and set at different times of year?

When a house is sited properly,
it will seem to belong naturally to the
land and be inseparable from it.

In too many recently built houses, the relation between site and house is completely ignored.

Then gradually move in closer. Start to notice the path of the road or street as it nears the property. What's the first thing you see? Is it a great big maple tree? The backside of a neighbor's garage? Get even closer until you're looking at the smallest details of the land: a slightly sloped grade, bits of ledge poking through the pine needles, or maybe a natural swale that still looks soggy. This process is what I call "the flyover." When I look at a piece of land for the first time, I imagine myself flying over it, absorbing the whole landscape—woods, hills, streams, roads, adjacent homes, and neighborhoods. I soak up the whole site. Then gradually, like a bird, I circle lower and lower, looking for the place to perch.

Whether you actually fly over the land (which is not a bad idea in some cases) or do it in your imagination with the plot plan spread out in front of you, the flyover will get you thinking about some basic qualities of the site. You'll learn where the sun will rise and set at different times of the year. If there are other houses in the neighborhood, the flyover will help you see how they might block or enhance your views. Similarly, if a site is surrounded by vacant lots, this is the time to think about where houses or other structures might be built someday. Ask questions now. When an excavator shows up next door, it will be too late.

Take notice of the vegetation, especially trees, at this stage. Keep in mind that deciduous trees lose their leaves in the winter,

SUNRISE, SUNSET

The first thing to do when you look at a site map is to find the north arrow. Then turn the map 180 degrees, because south is the most important point on the compass when building in the Northern Hemisphere. Why? Because most of our sunlight comes from the southern sky.

It's not enough to know that the sun rises in the east, moves through the southern sky, and sets in the west, because it doesn't always rise and set at the same point, nor does it rise to the same height on the horizon every day. Where I live, near Boston, the sun rises south of east in the winter, but rises north of east in the summer. In winter, it rises only about 30 degrees above the horizon; but in summer, it rises to about 70 degrees. Knowing the precise track of the sun, you can create a house with eaves that keep the summer sun from beating into second-story dormers yet allow the winter sun to warm the most frequently used rooms. Keeping in mind the position of the sun at different times of year can add comfort, variety, and vitality to your home.

Building within Limits

Typical of many suburban lots, this property was once much larger—more than 4 acres—but because local zoning required only 2 acres for building, the owners split it up to create a new lot toward the rear of the property. Their new lot now had two different side-yard setbacks—a wetlands setback and a road easement—which left us with a difficult "building envelope" directly over a sloped area and with no two parallel sides.

We wanted to get as much sun as possible into each room, but we had strict limitations to work within. Instead of siting the house parallel to a road or lot lines, we rotated it away from the road, aligning the long side on an east–west axis so that most of the windows would be facing south, east, or west.

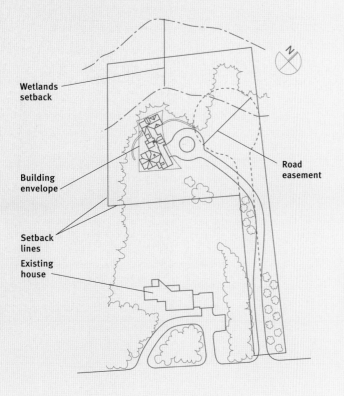

Every house occupies a broader landscape, **and taking both the natural and the man-made features of that landscape into consideration is essential when siting a house. This home was positioned on the site to capture the southern sunlight along the back, and existing trees were preserved to screen neighboring homes.**

The siting of the house plays off the regulatory limitations (as well as the location of a neighboring house) without sacrificing important qualities, such as sunlight.

This three-story home on a steep site might have looked too tall had it not been for the horizontal bands of color that define its exterior. The brick at the base, wood clapboards and battened panels in the midsection, and wood shingles on the roof mitigate the overall height, blending it into the surrounding landscape.

THE IMPORTANCE
OF FIRST IMPRESSIONS

*B*efore diving into the details of siting a house—taking measurements, calculating
setbacks, and checking elevations—I try to remain true to my initial impression of
the property. What struck me when I first saw it? What sort of a house came to mind?

After I've taken into account all the many influences involved in siting a house—sunlight, views, topography, privacy—
I begin to dream a bit, giving my first impressions room to grow.

In a very preliminary fashion, I begin to imagine what kind of house might look good on the site. Because for me, siting a house is more than just finding the best location; it also has to do with imagining the look of the house itself. Whether humble or grand, awe-inspiring, or just plain welcoming, a home's first impression is an important one. The more intimately linked with the site itself, the more it will seem just right.

exposing neighbors you never knew you had back in summer when you bought the property. Keep your eyes peeled for dips or rises in the land and outcrops of rock, and take special notice of wet areas on the site. Even if they don't involve regulatory approval, they'll be a nuisance unless properly graded and drained. Above all, consider the overall "feel" for the property—the sum of all these factors. I often come away from the flyover with a strong first impression—and with that, the design process has begun, if only subconsciously.

After the flyover, the next step is to think more specifically about how a house might fit into the environment. And while every site may be unique, there are *types* of sites. Rural sites with lots of acreage pose vastly different challenges than suburban sites on half-acre lots in the middle of a subdivision. (Both have unlimited potential, by the way.) Likewise, steep hillsides present a range of solutions that wouldn't even be considered for a flat site. A good place to begin thinking about the house design is to consider what type of site you're dealing with.

More Than Meets the Eye: The Rural Site

Figuring out where to put a house on a rural site can be more difficult than you might think. Sure, there are unlimited opportunities to rotate the house for sun and views, plus all the privacy you could ever want. Yet for those same reasons, a rural site can sometimes be the most challenging. If you have all the room you need, why one location over another? Sometimes restrictions on a smaller site, such as zoning setbacks, wetlands, and the houses nearby, can at least begin to set limits to where you should site your house. But a rural site is different. Where do you start?

I always start with the fundamentals: topography, climate, sun, and views. These are the factors you will live with every day, through every season, and for the most part they won't change, so

Figuring out where to put a house on a rural site can be more difficult than you might think.

The shapes of the two pavilions and the chimneys of this house blend naturally with the topography, vegetation, and even the distant hills on this rural site. The house was placed on a slight rise on the hilly property, giving it just enough height so that it doesn't appear to sink into the landscape, and yet it doesn't tower over the surroundings.

Small sites, even those on the water, pose challenges when it comes to views and sunlight because there are limited opportunities to rotate the buildings (site plan below). In this case, the winglike roof opened up the walls for bigger windows on both the first and the second floors, creating a one-and-a-half-story sitting area overlooking the best view toward the water (photo facing page). This is a case in which the site had a big impact on the final look of the house.

Overhanging sections of the second floor over the first offer protection against wind and rain, provide for a screened porch off one end of the house, and help enclose a deck.

planning around them is critical. But there are other considerations. Perhaps the property has unique features, such as a rock or ledge outcrop or a dense woodland. If you're lucky, the lot will be high and dry; but if it's wet, drainage will play a role in your siting decisions. There might be other buildings already on the property, like a barn, or perhaps there are artifacts, such as an old fence or stone wall, worth preserving even if it means sacrificing something else. Sometimes a preexisting right-of-way that must remain open can play a part in siting. Whatever the factors, each has to be balanced against the others as you marry your house to the land.

PLAYING OFF THE TOPOGRAPHY

Few homes sit on perfectly sculpted pieces of property just waiting for a structure to be dropped on it. Even the flattest site has some rise and fall in its topography, and a well-sited house will respond to these features. Often the topographical features of a lot are subtle—just a few feet of slope—but sometimes they can be dramatic. Because rural sites tend to have a fair amount of topographical variety, this is a major consideration, and it requires a lot of work and some imagination to exploit the nuances of a rural property.

How a structure plays off the site's topography can have a big impact. You don't need to be an architect to tell when a house fits

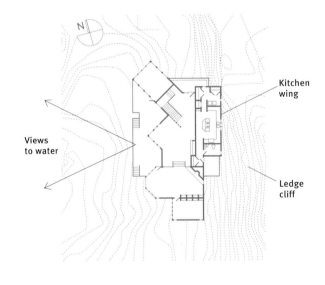

Kitchen wing

Views to water

Ledge cliff

A STEEP FIT

The elevation lines on this site drawing show how carefully the house was placed between a high cliff of ledge and the rocky coast. The long, linear shape of the kitchen wing aligns with the high cliff behind, while the rooms on the water side are angled to maximize views and sunlight.

Tailoring a House to a Hill

Consideration of site topography, sun, and vegetation can often lead to an unusual solution. This house, by architect James Cutler, is made up of a series of structures and rooms strung together into a compound of buildings. What's unique is that the line of buildings marches up a gradual incline and at the same time nestles quietly beside a dense third-growth forest. The architect broke apart the various functions of the house, connecting some and disconnecting others, all the while letting the house hug the slope.

The functions of the buildings also ascend metaphorically from arrival in the garage, past the greenhouse, through the mud-room, and into the living and sleeping areas of the house. As you move up the slope, you experience the forest to one side as a kind of enclosure and a bright, open meadow on the other, facing south. (For a photo of this house from the meadow, see the bottom photo on p. 45.) Had the topography been leveled, the wooded area not saved, or the meadow not cleared, the experience of this house would be dramatically different.

Out of deference to the environment, the roof of an exterior covered passageway accommodates a great tree that was on the property. Not all houses need to blend with the landscape so dramatically, but doing so creates a strong bond between the site and the buildings on it.

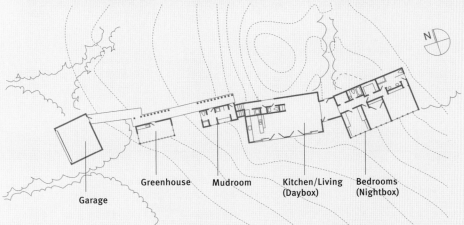

Garage Greenhouse Mudroom Kitchen/Living Bedrooms
(Daybox) (Nightbox)

The outdoor, covered passage nestles between forest and house. It bridges the natural and the man made, while occupying a break between the hills above and meadow below. By straddling these two features of the site, the house relates well to the land, while providing a sense of protection and enclosure.

A house that matches the local climate tends to blend in naturally with the landscape. The light, airy quality of this house—expressed through pavilion-like wings, porches, thin roof overhangs, trellises, and the transparency provided by windows aligned on both sides—is perfectly suited to its mild northern California climate.

the land and when it doesn't. A house can grip a steep slope or it can look as if it's in danger of sliding down the hill. As you look the site over, consider how topography will limit design decisions later. (For more on steep sites, see pp. 66–67.)

Exploiting a change in slope with a winding driveway or terraced porch can make the difference between an ordinary house and an extraordinary and distinctive one. Frank Lloyd Wright demanded site plans that showed every foot of elevation (a typical topographical survey shows elevation every 2 ft.). He understood

that the slightest change in slope could have a big effect on how a house relates to its site.

The best way to obtain topographical information about a piece of property is to hire a licensed surveyor or civil engineer to produce a plot plan. It should contain exact site boundaries and the rise and fall of the land. It can also show the location of existing structures, trees over a certain size, and other relevant regulatory information such as wetlands and deed restrictions. Once you've collected this information, go back and visit the site again. I'm amazed how much more a piece of property can actually rise or fall from what I might have first imagined in my flyover. It's all a part of getting to know your site before any ground is broken.

An open breezeway connects the living and bedroom wings and acts as a point of organization—and contemplation—for the entire property by linking the entry path and an old grove of oaks with the fields beyond (plan below).

RESPONDING TO REGION AND CLIMATE

As you explore a rural lot with the goal of building a house on it, it's important to consider climate—average temperatures, precipitation (including snow), and local information, such as the direction of the prevailing winds and the average number of sunny days in summer and in winter. I live in coastal New England, where the worst weather—blowing wind, rain, and snow—often comes off the ocean out of the northeast, not the northwest, as you might expect. In the summer, welcoming warm winds blow in from the southeast as often as from the southwest. (The closer to the coast the more pronounced this effect.) You may not be able to accommodate all the weather Mother Nature will throw your way, but it would be folly not to try to plan for the most common regional and local weather patterns.

Climate is an important consideration for any site, and the better a house can respond to its climate naturally, the more it will seem to belong. Many new houses don't have a unique look in part because they ignore the climate of their region. This hasn't always been true. In the eighteenth century, houses in the northeast had small exterior openings, large expanses of roof, and rooms arranged around a massive central chimney—all

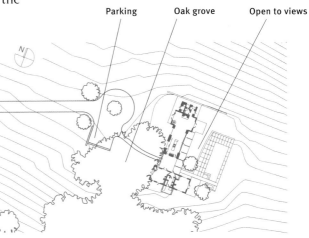

Parking   Oak grove   Open to views

RESPONDING TO THE SITE

Vegetation can have a big impact on a site. The oak grove provides a transition (and visual screening) between the driveway/parking area and the house. It shades some of the southern and western sun, complements the sloping topography, and leaves the north and east sides of the house wide open to the views.

Climate is an important consideration for any site, and the better a house can respond to its climate naturally, the more it will seem to belong.

Regional climate played a large part in determining the style of early New England houses. The small windows, large central chimney, and long, sweeping, north-facing roof all contributed to the popular seventeenth- and eighteenth-century "salt-box" style. The one element of ornamentation is on the chimney, signifying its importance functionally, aesthetically, and structurally.

to provide shelter and comfort in a harsh environment. Summer, not winter, is the extreme season in the south, and historic houses in this region were built with thin walls; open, airy central halls to circulate breezes; and deep, shady porches. Builders of the southwest adapted to their region by creating enclosed, covered patios that shaded the hot sun during the day and thick adobe walls to retain warmth during the cool evenings.

Since the late nineteenth century, our ability to heat, and later to cool, houses mechanically has made it easier to deal with weather extremes and, therefore, to build any style house anywhere in the country. As a result, house designs have become more uniform from region to region. It's the antithesis of distinctiveness. Worse, we're missing an opportunity to save energy by making houses that fit their climates rather than relying on sophisticated and expensive mechanical systems. The energy gained by extending a roof overhang to shield just enough of the high summer sun while admitting the lower winter sunlight, for example, is something to start thinking about even when you're sizing up the site. A distinctive house will respond to the climate and seem to belong to the site and the region in which it sits. In many ways, a distinctive, timeless design is the natural result of the thoughtful consideration of climate.

Climate dictated regional style differences in the days before air-conditioning. Southern houses of the nineteenth century, for example, had lots of windows for ventilation and wide overhangs to shade porches. They also employed luxurious trees and other plantings to provide cool shade naturally. These utilitarian design elements give antebellum homes much of their distinctive look.

Capturing sunlight and views

One great advantage of a rural site in the planning stage is the ability to move and rotate a house to capture sunlight and views. A house with lots of sunlight and good views is always more lively and pleasant to live in. You are more aware of the day and the seasons as the light changes from hour to hour and day to day in each room. An abundance of good light combined with a satisfying outlook (it doesn't have to be stunning, just pleasant to look at) can hold your attention and emphasize the importance of one room over another.

If sunlight is important to you, the question you need to ask yourself when looking at a rural lot is: Which way is south? This is so important that I carry a compass with me at all times. Why south? Because in the Northern Hemisphere, most direct sunlight comes from that direction, and it is sunlight that activates the spaces inside and outside a house. (The moon also appears in the southern sky when viewed from the Northern Hemisphere.) With a little extra care and some imagination (and, once again, some compromises), it is quite possible to create a floor plan in which sunlight can enter every room in the house, not just those along the south side.

Large, steeply pitched rooflines are common in northern climates where heavy snowfalls are the norm. The simple but powerful roof protects against the harsh Canadian climate but also sits lightly on a series of piers, giving the house a distinct rhythm day or night.

Rather than shield the house from the sun, this roof tilts up toward an open meadow, allowing the large expanses of glass to capture maximum sunlight in the often-overcast Pacific Northwest. Deciduous trees and large overhangs help shade the house from hot summer sun.

TRUE NORTH

True north is the actual direction of the north meridian from any given point on a piece of property. Magnetic north is north as indicated by the magnetic needle of a compass. There's a difference—known as the *deviation*—and the deviation changes, depending on your position on the earth. In Boston, the compass will point about 16 degrees west of true north, whereas in San Francisco, the compass will point 17 degrees east of true north. In the past, site surveys would indicate the difference by a more ornate tail on the true north arrow, but you don't see that designation much any more. If it's not clear on a site plan or map, be sure to ask; a few degrees can have a big effect on the natural light that washes into a room.

The effect of sunlight on indoor spaces is powerful and transforming. The continuous band of windows, facing east, south, and west makes lighting the rooms almost unnecessary during the day, no matter what time of year.

With a wide umbrella-like roof—seemingly held up by the massive central chimney—over an almost completely transparent space, the house welcomes sunlight into nearly every room in early morning and late afternoon.

Even if sunlight in every room isn't the goal, I try to position the longest side of a house within 30 degrees of due south. This means that most of the rooms of the house will get some direct sunlight during some portion of the day. In certain circumstances, depending on the shape of the house or the views, I may rotate the long axis as much as 45 degrees from south, but only reluctantly—it's not worth the potential loss of sunlight. Strictly adhering to this rule can lead to contradictions and compromises. The best views may not be in a southerly direction, for example. Nevertheless, south is the most important point on your compass.

Sunlight, views, and topography are all related. The best siting for your house might not always be out in the open with full sun, on a flat site, with the best views all around. You may have to optimize one site asset over the other, depending on which opportunity you want to exploit and which you can live without. The topography may block some sun or views, or the best sun might come from the opposite direction of the best views. Few sites are perfect, and having to balance topography, sun, and views is a common problem.

PRESERVING WHAT MAKES THE SITE SPECIAL

Siting a house on a rural piece of land doesn't just mean taking inventory of the topography, climate, sun, and views and then finding a place to pour the foundation. As you get deeper into the siting process, you may start to overlook qualities of the property that made you select it in the first place. Go back to the flyover, dig up any notes you made on the plot plan, and try to recall what impressions you had that made the site special.

Sometimes people want protection from the sun. At one end of this house, facing west, the area under a large roof overhang encloses a shaded and screened sitting area.

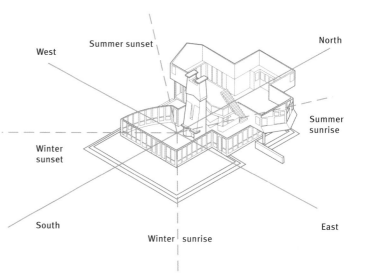

FANNING TO THE SUNLIGHT

By siting the long axis of the house within 15 degrees of due south, all the major interior and exterior spaces have some direct sun at some time during the day, with some seasonal variations.

Taking Stock

This house in Maine on a rural waterfront lot is a good example of first taking inventory and then synthesizing all the features of a site that make it special before deciding where to put the house. First, the architects gathered all relevant information—topography, sun, views, existing road and house, wet areas, prominent trees, rocky areas, soil conditions, and coastal setback lines. A second pass filtered the initial inventory, identifying elements they wanted to preserve or enhance. View, setback, high rock, low spot, special area, special vegetation, and even a special oak were important features worth preserving. As a result of this synthesis, the architects and owners identified a "prime building area."

This doesn't yet pinpoint the exact location for the new house, but it does describe approximately where the house would best be located. Later on, the site analysis also helps define the house plans and elevations.

A site analysis doesn't plot the specific location of the foundation, driveway, or outbuildings. Instead it's a process of first taking inventory of everything from topography to vegetation and views.

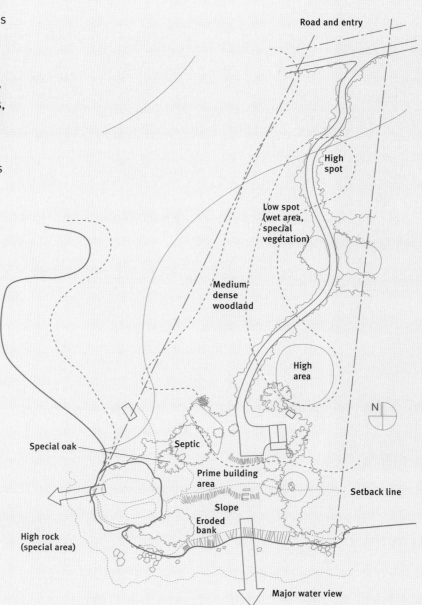

Road and entry

High spot

Low spot (wet area, special vegetation)

Medium-dense woodland

High area

N

Special oak

Septic

Prime building area

Setback line

Slope

Eroded bank

High rock (special area)

Major water view

Long and rectangular, with carefully placed windows, this house humbly defers to the landscape.

The long side of the house doesn't face the water but rather sits perpendicular so it doesn't block the view from the rest of the property, suggesting (intentionally) that what is outside the house is just as important.

Mixing new and old helps unite house and site. An old stone foundation wall was preserved in the entry court and interior entryway. Not only does it provide a distinctive visual touch in a contemporary home but it roots the home to the land and the region in a unique way.

This small barnlike house sits partially within and on top of an old stone foundation wall that was discovered on the property. While it need not be so literal, blending the new with the old is a good way to make a house look like it belongs.

THE SUBURBAN LOT

The terms rural *and* urban *are usually clear—one is in the country, the other in the city. But because so much of our* landscape is a blend of small towns, large towns, and clusters of housing, neither rural nor urban, a precise definition of *suburban* is elusive. It really comes down to the density of the housing rather than our predetermined images of what constitutes country or city, and there are no hard-and-fast definitions. When I refer to a suburban site, I'm thinking of properties roughly between ¼ acre and 2 acres near large metropolitan areas. Of course, a lot this size surrounded by 5,000 acres of pasture would qualify as rural—even if it is within a short drive of a city or small town.

A vacant property will look quite different when a building is erected on it, so it's worth making a list of features to preserve or enhance before the excavators and bulldozers arrive. Sometimes a unique feature of the site can be incorporated into the design of a house, such as a graceful stand of trees, a forgotten stone wall, a barn, or some other outbuilding (see the photos above). Of course, the compromises continue. There may be a beautiful tree just where you think it might be best to place a deck, or an outcrop of rock may stand in the way of the driveway. But these natural and man-made artifacts carry with them a sense of history, something worth preserving into the future along with the new.

The Site Next Door

The qualities that make houses on rural sites so appealing—lots of sunlight, great views, a familial relationship to the land—can also be had on modestly sized sites in more populated areas. More often than not, houses are built on "the site next door," by which I mean a relatively small lot (¼ acre or less up to 2 acres) in a typical

The elegant and private quality of the separate guest wing is a tribute to a careful site analysis and design. Such a space would not have been possible with a more typical neighborhood side yard.

As unusual as the shapes of this house are, they make sense in the context of the neighborhood on Lake Michigan. The curved guest wing grants some privacy from the neighbors, carves out an intimate courtyard, and allows the family wing of the house (photo p. 52) to have an unobstructed view to the lake. This would have been difficult had the design been rectilinear.

suburban or semirural neighborhood. The vast majority of single-family homes are built in these types of neighborhoods, usually next to existing houses or new houses that are being (or are about to be) built. The proximity of other houses can have a considerable influence on the site design of a new house. Just a small setback or rotation of a new house might make a big difference in outdoor space or interior privacy.

Thoughtful siting is just as important—if not more so—in a typical development as it is on a rural site, because of the impact a house will have on the larger neighborhood (and vice versa). Imagine, for example, if every other house in a typical suburban subdivision was placed farther back on its lot (even within existing setback requirements). Everyone on the street would have better views from their side windows, not to mention the communal benefit of variety that the whole neighborhood could enjoy. And who hasn't complained about the cookie-cutter nature of house placement these days? It doesn't have to be that bad. I tell clients who are considering lots in subdivisions to take heart. Knowing beforehand what is already near or around you can inform your siting choices. See it as an advantage, not a drawback.

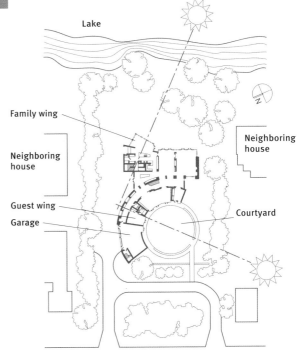

A ROUND PEG IN A SQUARE HOLE

The path of the sun shows how the rooms, arranged around the perimeter of this house, capture the sun as it travels through the sky from east to west. The floor plan is a direct response to the rising and setting sun and the need to create a sense of private space and views in a densely populated neighborhood.

The family wing, along the more private back side of the house, faces the lake, with wide open glass walls to take in the view. This contrasts with the more private guest wing that faces the street.

SETBACKS

Setbacks—the distances that a structure has to be "set back" from the lot lines—are the first thing you need to look for when buying a piece of property, especially for small lots in urban or suburban settings. Setbacks are typically a certain dimension in feet from the front, side, and rear lot lines (usually the front and rear setbacks are larger than the side yard setbacks) and circumscribe the foundation line of a house, often with exceptions made for decks, bays, eaves, or other overhangs.

Sometimes you never reach the setbacks, but in many smaller lots, setbacks will create major limitations in the size and orientation of a house. Towns initiated setbacks to keep people from building too close to the street or their neighbors, although restrictions like these are currently being questioned, because many towns want to discourage sprawl and encourage more densely populated neighborhoods. Also, many people have a desire to return to the days of front porches and back alleys, which setbacks often render impossible. When a lot is particularly tight, you might try for a little extra room through a variance with the local zoning board. But variances typically require a public hearing in which all your neighbors have a chance to object. Depending on what you are proposing, it might not be a good way to start out in a new neighborhood.

There are many factors to consider when placing your house on a site next door. As with rural sites, topography, sun, and views are important considerations. But unlike a rural site, it's perhaps most important to consider the character of the houses nearby and those immediately next door. Will the houses next door block your views, shield your sun or the prevailing winds, or detract from your privacy? If there are no existing houses, find out if there might be some day. Some simple research can tell you whether the lots next door are privately or publicly owned or if there are any future building restrictions.

It's also worth paying close attention to other structures, such as garages and sheds. It's no fun having to look at your neighbors coming and going all day long. Because privacy is hard won on small suburban lots, topography becomes extremely important. Flat sites might need an outbuilding, fencing, or plantings to get some privacy from the neighbors, while sloped sites may have built-in screening possibilities, and sometimes better views. Look too at the existing trees, shrubs, and vegetation. Imagine what your lot or the lot next door would look like with or without some or all of it.

Deferring to the Neighborhood

Siting a house in an existing neighborhood or subdivision ultimately has implications beyond your own property line. How much should a newcomer nod to the houses already there? I always lean toward deferring to the existing neighborhood styles, at least in some way, because I think fitting in promotes a better sense of community as well as a sense of timelessness. This doesn't mean that every house in the neighborhood has to be the same—that would be boring. It's more that each house seems to be speaking in the same language, using the same vocabulary. In architecture, like the spoken word, you can speak the same language but say different things.

Some of my favorite neighborhoods are those in which the houses seem to both fit in and stand out simultaneously. The houses in these neighborhoods, built and rebuilt over many generations, loosely conform to an overall style yet individually maintain a unique identity. The houses are *variations* on the theme. And

Siting a house in an existing neighborhood or subdivision has implications beyond your own property line.

Even in a densely packed neighborhood, a house can simultaneously fit in and stand out on a site. This house on Martha's Vineyard shares a vocabulary—the shapes and textures—with its larger neighbors and the locale. The windows are placed to gain as much sunlight and view as possible, and that feature in itself, while a practical consideration, gives it a one-of-a-kind feel.

An Old Building Becomes a New Site

Siting decisions are not limited to suburban or rural sites. This house was literally carved out of an existing industrial building on the site, with pieces of the old building being demolished to open up the courtyard garden and admit more light. The new building consists of a retail space on the first floor, a rental apartment on the second, and a townhouse apartment for the owner on the third and fourth floors. It wraps around a garden of lawn, stone paths, flowerbeds, planters, and trellises—a natural sanctuary within an urban setting. (It took a great leap of faith on the part of the homeowner to give up valuable floor space in return for a garden.)

The walls are mostly glass, twisting at different angles to gain better views of the garden and to create a variety of indoor spaces, each of which has its own outlook and natural lighting. The architects created a site where none existed. Imagine how wonderful New York City would be if more hidden worlds such as this existed behind the street walls.

Stucco, steel, and glass **are a nice material complement to the predominant brick structures in this New York neighborhood.**

The exterior wall zigs and zags its way around the open garden in an effort to maximize natural light and offer a variety of views. Because it was impossible to have most of the windows face south, the architects took advantage of reflected sunlight off the garden courtyard.

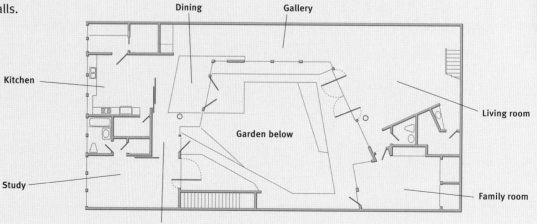

Dining Gallery
Kitchen
Living room
Garden below
Study
Family room
Entry foyer

Responding to site influences, especially in an urban setting, can often have exciting results. View and sun were made possible by removing a portion of the existing building. Rather than follow the convention of making the exterior walls flat, they jut out at different angles, capturing the sun at different times of day and enlivening the spaces inside with a variety of light and views.

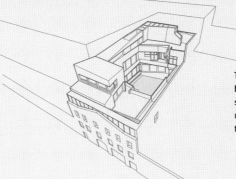

The rear of the townhouse steps back and down, allowing as much sun as possible into the garden. The upper terrace next to the street has the potential for sun all day long.

The unusual shape of the curved roof is an alternative to the flat roofs everywhere else in the neighborhood. But even though it sets the house apart, it also fits in against the wind-blown vegetation. Inside, the curved roof has an almost nautical flavor, appropriate considering the views of San Francisco Bay beyond (photo below).

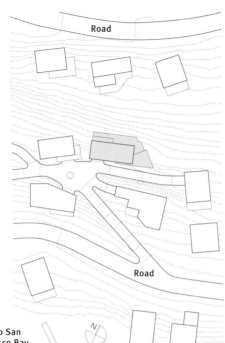

THE VIEW FROM THE HILL

At first glance, it would seem that many of the views from this house would be blocked by the neighbors. But raising the house and taking advantage of the relatively steep slope maximizes sun, views, and ventilation.

there's a great deal of variety. What's happened is that (for the most part) each new addition to the neighborhood has somehow managed to fit in just enough not to disrupt the theme. Some neighborhoods have no perceptible theme or style—or they may have a style you dislike—but if at all possible, try to discover that theme and play off it.

Another goal when siting a house in a neighborhood is to balance public and private spaces. Should the house join the neighborhood by standing exposed to the street, or should it turn its back on the neighbors in favor of a more private environment, hiding itself behind walls, fences, or plantings? A distinctive house balances these two impulses—it will defer and stand out simultaneously, capturing privacy without hiding from the world. People hold these kinds of houses and neighborhoods dearly to their hearts, and rightly so, because there is a greater sense of community generated by that kind of neighborhood deferral.

This house respects its neighborhood by deferring in style to many of the houses around it. It also asks us to respect its privacy by showing you its side, not its face. A stone wall and wood fence partially screen the house from the street.

A taller, single house with lots of yard would have worked on this site; but by splitting the house into three sections and folding them inward, away from the street, the architects created a smaller, more private and intimate courtyard with lots of sun.

MAKING THE MOST OF SUN, VIEWS, AND PRIVACY

Getting great sunlight, creating views, and carving out a little privacy in a neighborhood filled with other houses can introduce a host of compromises. Everyone loves windows and light, but openings also make it easier for neighbors to see inside (or at least give the people inside the feeling that they have less privacy). But even the most private people don't want to live in a bunker. Balancing all these goals—or at least planning for them—is something that must begin with siting.

When houses are lined up side by side and facing each other across a road, the siting options may seem limited. But there may be ways to place the house on the lot to exploit all the possibilities. One simple approach—so simple I'm surprised more people don't do it—is to place the house on the lot where it makes the most sense rather than mimicking the placement of the existing houses. It might mean choosing between a big backyard and more distance from the street, but rotating a house away from neighbors can open up a more private view. Another option is to use the shape of the house to create private indoor and outdoor spaces where none existed before. The house can thus shield itself.

Place the house on the lot where it makes the most sense rather than mimicking the placement of the existing houses.

Neighborhood Improvement

Located in San Francisco's Noe Valley, this single-family residence on a double lot was designed to work with an existing garden that runs the length of the site with mature maple and pine trees and hedges. The long side of the house fronts onto the garden side. Several variances were required that traded rear-yard for side-yard setbacks, but in a situation that is unusual in San Francisco, the project received unanimous neighborhood support because the garden-like side yard allowed open space to be visually shared by the rest of the built-up neighborhood.

The house is organized in a barbell scheme with the living room, family room, and upstairs bedrooms located in smaller gabled forms facing the garden at each end. These smaller-scale "houses" are connected by a large light-filled gallery and porch that opens out to the garden and also contains the kitchen, hallway, and bathrooms. Materials were kept simple with painted trim and moldings reminiscent of the earlier houses in the neighborhood.

A large light-filled gallery and porch opens out to the garden and steps back and up from the lawn to allow dramatic views from all the spaces it connects.

From overall site planning to room proportions to detailing, this project was designed to fit in and enhance the existing qualities already found in the neighborhood.

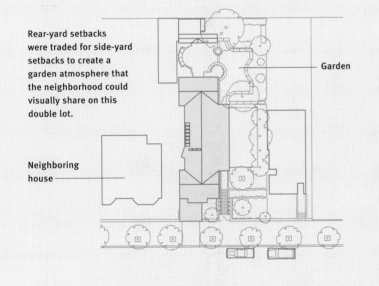

Rear-yard setbacks were traded for side-yard setbacks to create a garden atmosphere that the neighborhood could visually share on this double lot.

Garden

Neighboring house

Good planning—and some variances—resulted in a pleasing garden that could be enjoyed by the whole neighborhood.

Even in a dense urban or suburban neighborhood, proper planning can enhance sun, views, and privacy.

SITE SKETCH

The first thing I do when confronted with a lot is to map out everything I know about the site: neighboring houses, direction of sun and wind, good or bad views, and any other factor that I think could possibly inform my choices about where to put a house (and, later, what type of house to build). I do this by producing a rough site sketch that I can refer to as I make siting decisions. The sketch may not be accurate or even to scale, but it is the starting point for all the design decisions I will make later on, not just about the site, but the plan and exterior elevations as well (as seen in the drawing on the facing page).

The garage shields the neighbor's house and helps define a clear distinction between the formal entrance at left and the informal entry door at right.

Placing a new house in an existing neighborhood is sometimes a blessing, because you know in advance what your options are for sun, views, and privacy. If there are no houses in the area yet, find out if there might be some day, and where on the lot they are likely to be placed. Some simple research can tell you what building restrictions, such as setbacks, are likely to be in force.

A house our firm designed for a suburban lot in Massachusetts (photos below and facing page) takes an unconventional approach to deal with all the problems and opportunities the site presented. The obvious place to put the house would have been parallel and facing the road—like most houses in subdivisions. But there's no reason why a new house should always parallel the road or any other property line. Instead, we placed the house at the edge of the woods and rotated it away from the road. This placement left views into the woods and enough room for a small circular driveway in front that gives the house a more stately look and at the same time lets more morning sun into the front of the house. But it also gave us a chance to carve out a little privacy. The garage blocks the view of the neighboring house—and because the garage faces north, we didn't sacrifice much sunlight in the process.

Lots of windows and a screened porch on the rear of the house take advantage of the view to the woods and pond to the south. The rear and more private side of the house has noticeably more glass than the more public front facade.

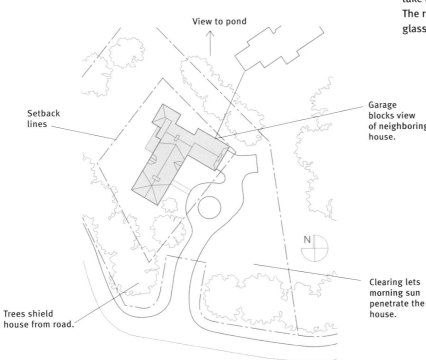

View to pond

Setback lines

Garage blocks view of neighboring house.

Clearing lets morning sun penetrate the house.

Trees shield house from road.

N

TURNED AWAY FROM THE STREET

Rather than lining up parallel with the street, this house is turned away, giving the owners more privacy. The skewed placement also left room for an elegant driveway—without having to cut down too many trees. The curved driveway makes the house, not the garage, the first thing you see.

Who says a porch has to be close to the ground? This fire tower–like porch takes in a stunning and dramatic view.

Perching over wooden piers on a stone wall, the house hovers above the property for incredible views over the valley. The continuous stone base seems to grow out of the site, helping to anchor the house in a fitting way.

Difficult and Dramatic Sites

Rural and suburban sites are the most common properties out there for new construction. But sometimes a site can be more challenging. In many high-growth areas, all the really good sites are taken. If you are looking for good schools, a short commute, or some other amenity in high demand, you may find yourself figuring out a way to salvage a lot that most people passed over for something better.

Among those lots passed over you will inevitably come across a difficult steep site that scared away many a homeowner (and even a few builders). They're not the easiest to build on, but their biggest flaw (their steepness) is also their greatest opportunity for distinctiveness in the form of interesting level changes or spectacular views. Dramatic locations, such as water sites, may not seem all that challenging because the view is pretty obvious (and unobstructed), but they, too, require special considerations precisely because of their proximity to the water's edge. One of my most satisfying pleasures as an architect is to design for challenging sites that call out for creative solutions.

House

VIEWS FROM ABOVE

This tiny, 1,000-sq.-ft. house sits high on a wooded cliff in West Virginia, overlooking a river 300 ft. below. Each one of the three parts, or pavilions, has its own vantage point.

River

SALVAGING THE LESS-THAN-PERFECT LOT

During the various building booms that have occurred in this country over the last 50 years, less-than-perfect sites in every neighborhood have been passed over in favor of those that could be built on without much trouble. I built my first house on just such a passed-over site almost 20 years ago (see the photo and plan at right). As such lots go, it wasn't bad. It was a small site (about ½ acre) at the end of a dead-end road, facing south in a small-scaled neighborhood. No one wanted to build on it because the town zoning required a variance for lack of proper street frontage. I took up the challenge because the qualities of the lot far outweighed the effort required to get the variance. My petition with the town (and appeal to the neighbors) was successful, and I lived there for more than 15 years.

There are a number of lots like these still available in every town. As sprawl becomes more of an issue and smart-growth initiatives are taken up as its antidote, lots once passed over for whatever reason are becoming more popular and more valuable.

Sometimes a site is passed over because it was abandoned. It may once have had a house on it, or it may even have been used for commercial purposes. Such sites are often overgrown or are otherwise deteriorating. If you find such a site, look it over carefully. Walk around and through it and do a little research into its history. You may be surprised to find that it has more amenities than you first imagined.

Many less-than-perfect sites aren't unbuildable—they're just underused. Some already have a house on them, but there may be better spots for the foundation. It can be hard to see, but simply rebuilding on a different spot can

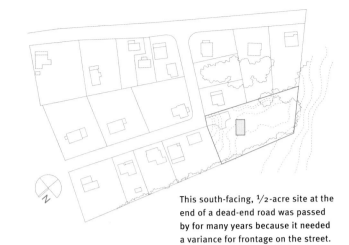

This south-facing, ½-acre site at the end of a dead-end road was passed by for many years because it needed a variance for frontage on the street.

This 1,150-sq.-ft. house tucked into a ½-acre (above) achieves a good deal of privacy by turning its back to the street. At the same time, the south facade opens up to sun. The siting allows for a better view, too, because the house was pushed toward the front lot line, leaving more yard in back.

Marrying New and Old

This site, found by James Estes, an architect in Rhode Island, was once a commercial greenhouse complex that had been abandoned in the 1950s. The overgrown tangle of steel, broken glass, and concrete was surrounded by wetlands, which drained into a small pond used for watering plants and feeding the greenhouse's steam boiler.

The lot was zoned for both commercial and residential construction, and it was large (4 acres) and private because it was the last lot on a dead-end street. Given the adjoining wetlands, the site had a relatively small buildable area and had, therefore, remained undeveloped. And the extensive ruins, rubble, and overgrowth made it almost impenetrable when Estes found it. Amid this tangle, the architect saw an opportunity. The new house occupies the northern edge of the former greenhouse footprint and uses the long area to the south—now cleared of all the ruins save one—as a private outdoor area with southern exposure. In warm seasons, the whole house opens up to become a continuous screen porch.

Instead of placing the house in the middle of the site, the architect pushed it toward the front, opening up a large expanse of property facing south, which meant more natural light.

Mixing old and new helps tie a house to its site in an intimate way. A remnant of the greenhouse stands as both an interesting view from the house and a reminder of the site's past.

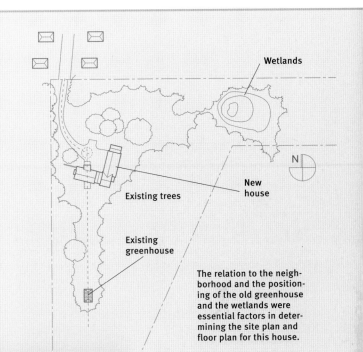

Wetlands

Existing trees

New house

Existing greenhouse

N

The relation to the neighborhood and the positioning of the old greenhouse and the wetlands were essential factors in determining the site plan and floor plan for this house.

By forming an ell and providing fewer windows on the north side, this house is not only environmentally sound but has a clearly defined entry point and a better sense of privacy.

Steep sites call for tall buildings. You need a certain amount of height to get out into the light, and footprints tend to be more economical when they are compact. The unusual, tall character of this exterior is a direct response to the compact and steep site.

sometimes redeem a second-rate site. Houses that were poorly sited to begin with often also lack any distinctive qualities.

When I'm scouting an underused site, I try to look past the buildings and sum up the site's potential as if there were nothing there but the natural environment. Then I assess whether I could renovate the house or whether it makes more sense just to tear it down and start over with an entirely new site plan.

Another type of underused site is one that has a good existing house on it, but because the site is so large there is a potential to split off another buildable lot. If you think you've found such a lot, I'd suggest going to the local municipal offices and finding out who owns it. Sometimes if you approach a lot owner with a sensible proposal, they will listen. These two possibilities represent a huge number of potential building sites.

THE STEEP SITE

Steep sites often are passed over because, at first glance, they seem the most difficult (and expensive) to build on. But you'd be surprised how well an imaginative designer and a savvy builder can sneak a perfectly charming home onto a staggeringly steep lot. There are some physical limitations, though. For instance, driveways by code generally can't exceed a 12 percent slope—they

HEIGHT HAS ITS LIMITATIONS

Almost every city and town has height restrictions, and for obvious reasons. Who wants a neighbor to build a 10-story house? Towns usually limit houses to 35 ft. from grade. But here's the catch: What is "grade"? Some towns define grade as the average grade of the land *after* construction. Others define it as average grade *before* construction. Some definitions use *mean grade* as a yardstick. It's important to know the difference.

Average grade is determined by adding a series of grade elevations along a foundation line and dividing by the number in the series. Mean grade is the midpoint between the high and low grade elevations along the foundation wall. The average and mean can be the same, but they can also be different. Variances from these requirements are possible but are often difficult to obtain. I always try to stay within the regulations in the first place. It's a whole lot easier.

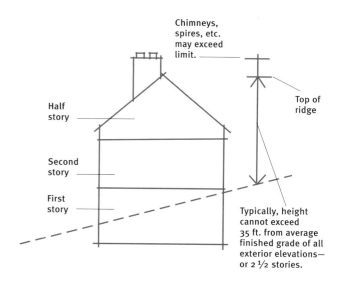

Chimneys, spires, etc. may exceed limit.

Half story

Second story

First story

Top of ridge

Typically, height cannot exceed 35 ft. from average finished grade of all exterior elevations— or 2 ½ stories.

would be too difficult to drive on or plow in bad weather. Vegetation doesn't grow well on more than a 30 percent slope, so erosion is a concern. Grading, setting foundations, and easily accessing floor levels can also be difficult. And because most cities and towns limit the height of houses to approximately 35 ft. above the average grade, it can even sometimes be difficult to rise high enough above grade on all sides of the house on a steep site.

A steep site on a small lot can be difficult because its steepness doesn't allow you to adjust the house much for sun, views, or privacy. But steep sites can present opportunities as well. They can actually provide better sun, views, ventilation, and more privacy from higher floor levels than you might typically have on a flatter site. Such sites are unique, and if handled with imagination, can produce a house that you can't find anywhere else.

THE WATER SITE

Siting a house on the water seems like the easiest job around. After all, you know where the focus is going to be, and the more spectacular the view, the better, right? Well, it's not always so simple. Water sites—on lakes, rivers, oceans, or even ponds—can be no-brainers or the most difficult situation you will ever encounter. Flooding, glare, wind-driven rain, extreme temperature changes, insects, and exposure to other harsh conditions are the norm. Most water sites also come with a raft of wetland regulations, ranging from rules enforced by municipal authorities to state and federal laws. These regulations, depending on the house's proximity to water, can have a major impact on the design of the house, affecting not just the siting but also the view.

Many less-than-perfect sites aren't unbuildable—they're just underused.

Water, grass, stone wall, and natural-colored house materials make an appropriate palette for this water site.

Difficult but Dramatic

I've designed many summer and year-round homes on waterfront sites, each posing its own challenges. One of them, in Gloucester, Massachusetts, illustrates how even the most restrictive building environment can lead to creative solutions. The house had to be built behind a parallel line 100 ft. back from the water's edge, and additional zoning regulations required setbacks from the street, resulting in a long and narrow footprint. At first, this might have seemed like a huge disadvantage—only one side of the house would capture the spectacular ocean views. But then we started to look at it as an opportunity to make a more interesting plan.

The living room, kitchen, and master bedroom all have great views, the other rooms less so, and the entry has no view at all. In fact, when you enter the house, you're not even aware of the view. This has its own logic—giving it all away at once would be like having the main course before the appetizer. It may seem contradictory, but keeping one area of the house completely boxed off from the site was the way to take full advantage of it.

Another challenge was the rocky coastline. Rather than blast away a large portion of rock to fashion a level site, we decided instead to take away as little ledge as possible. This means that the floor steps down from the entry to the living levels over the rocky slope toward the water. The study, living/dining room, and decks are just two steps up form the rocks. The result is a house that seems to fit naturally on its site, from inside and out.

The rectangular plan of this house, parallel to the water's edge, was determined largely by regulatory setbacks from both the water's edge and the street, but it also resulted in good views for the most important rooms.

Living room

Deck   Kitchen

On the interior, stepping down gradually over the rocky, existing topography leads to a breathtaking living space.

The angular shapes of the roofs reflect and blend with the jagged quality of the rocky shoreline below.

The exterior deck steps down gradually over the length of the house, responding to the changes in topography and culminating with a plateau of useful ledge to sit on.

One advantage of placing the house parallel to the water is that many rooms—in this case the kitchen—have a dramatic view to the rocky coast and ocean edge below.

Siting a house on the water seems like the easiest job around...but it's not always so simple.

These three "sibling" cottages on the Maine coast are connected by a rambling deck. Each cottage has its own living/sleeping spaces and each looks at a slightly different view toward the water, one of the benefits of a compound approach to siting.

The instinct to build close to the water always has to be tempered by the knowledge that the living conditions will be extreme. Hot sun, flooding, blowing wind, rain, and salt spray from the ocean are just some of the potential enemies. How close to the water is *too* close? Regulations establish some limits, such as the minimum distance from a body of water or the allowable height above water level. But keep in mind that these regulations are not foolproof. There are many situations where the law lets you build too close for some people's comfort.

When I look at a waterfront lot, I try to balance the potential for exposure with the need for enclosure, protection, and durability. If the homeowner likes to sit outside a lot, I'd be sure to allow for one or more generous decks, but I'd also suggest a mitigating element, such as large roof overhangs to protect against extreme sun, wind, or weather that may not be so enjoyable. Likewise, if I maximize views with expanses of glass, I'd be sure to use only the best windows with insulated glass, storm panels, or triple glazing to make sure they hold up under the worst conditions. Water sites also require that you pay special attention to siding and roofing materials. But sometimes dealing with these kinds of problems can result in a distinctive look, such as a unique siding pattern or a crisper-looking roof.

A House of the Site

Whether the property is an outcrop over the Atlantic or a modest parcel on a winding suburban road, the goal in siting a house is to integrate the structure with the land, buildings, and natural features around it. Sometimes it's straightforward, other times it takes some creativity to achieve this union of new and old, man-made and natural. Siting a

The spaces between each cottage (photo, facing page) provide outdoor rooms of different scale and character for private and large gatherings, each with its own private view. Spreading buildings out takes up more space on a site, but it also creates opportunities to marry the house to the land.

house can often take the form of pushing and pulling, as you search to find the best way to make the marriage work.

There is little salvation for a house that ignores the land around it. Some work, but others look like lost tourists plopped down in an unfamiliar landscape, hoping to blend in but hopelessly standing out. Unfortunately, the solution to haphazard or just plain ridiculous siting choices are somewhat limited. New windows or a change of color won't do the trick. It's like sitting in an uncomfortable chair—no matter how much you wiggle around in it, you'll still be uncomfortable. Once you understand the site fully and come to some conclusion about positioning your house, the next step is to begin defining the house plan itself.

Salvaging a Lot Passed Over

FOR ALMOST 100 YEARS, this site on a hill in New Hampshire sat vacant. Anyone who came to look at it just turned around and walked away. And for good reason. The site was so steep that a driveway would have exceeded a 12 percent slope in places, which meant the owners would need a variance, and the zoning board was not known for its generosity in handing them out.

There were other obstacles. Because the land had been used for farming for years before it lay fallow, there was a zon-

A long, steep drive finds its way to the plateau at the highest point on the site.

The more private south side of the house explodes with glass to capture light, views, and breezes. The most-used rooms of the house, including the living and dining area and master bedroom wing, share the best views.

ing requirement that limited the amount of property that could be disturbed for building. The rest of the parcel was, in effect, governed by a conservation easement, which meant the owners would later be prevented from building anywhere outside the house footprint. Of course, this wasn't a huge drawback—3 acres of the 4-acre parcel were too steep for any building anyway.

But steepness is a virtue as well as a curse. At the top of the slope, covered over with brush and saplings, was an almost perfectly level plateau that, with imagination, could be a stunning site with great views and light. So the prospective buyers didn't give up. With a little research, they discovered that the sellers had been paying taxes on the property as if it had been a buildable lot. The buyers used this in their appeal to the zoning board: If the sellers had been paying taxes all those years on a buildable lot, then the town ought to allow them to build on it, right?

The buyers prevailed. With luck, imagination, and a great deal of fortitude (including 13 town hearings), the zoning board granted their appeals. The new owners were able to buy a piece of property that no one wanted, and it was worth it. It was high, flat where it needed to be, faced south, had great ventilation, and

The driveway approaches the hidden, almost secretive north side of the house, which has few windows. Pushing the house toward one edge of the buildable area opened up room for a level lawn in front.

The central hall continues the path of the driveway and ends up at the living hall, a high-ceilinged and bright living/dining space that is the heart of the plan.

The broad shingle roof is interrupted only occasionally by dormers and gables (and here by the unusual "slotted" gable). There is no framing or trim visible at the roof edge, creating a crisp line around the perimeter.

had a beautiful view of the Connecticut River valley.

As with many challenging sites, we took advantage of the most difficult aspect of the site—its steepness—and turned it into one of the very features that make the house distinctive. The driveway climbs a long, steep trail and faces away from the house as it reaches the top of the hill, then turns back toward the house, giving visitors a nice surprise when they make that last turn. And because the hill was flat with a north/south orientation, we were able to position the floor plan for

The kitchen, with its own bay window **facing east, is at the crossroads between the entry, the living hall, and the screened porch.**

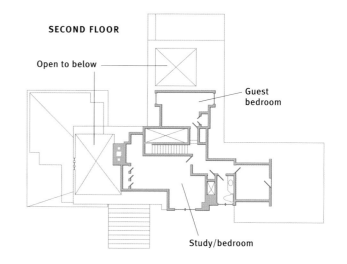

Porches are opportunities to add variety. **With a curved lead-coated copper roof (top photo facing page) and tongue-and-groove interior woodwork, the screened porch has its own fanciful quality that sets it apart—but not too much apart.**

maximum sun and views. Rather than center the house in the middle of the plateau, we pushed it toward the edge, leaving enough room for a south-facing lawn while enhancing the drama of the site.

An Informal Floor Plan

A good floor plan follows easily from a good site plan; the two ought to be integrated. In this floor plan, one literally leads to the other. Whether you arrive through the garage or the front door, you move into a central hallway that continues in the direction of the driveway toward the southern exposure. It's as if the driveway, and the land itself, continued into the house. The final destination—a high, light-filled room—is the end of the journey. This is the reward, like reaching the summit of a mountain and taking in the view. The house actually became part of the hill.

The floor plan is an informal but traditional one, a plan that could easily fulfill

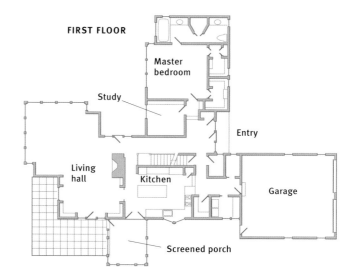

FIRST FLOOR

Master bedroom

Study

Entry

Living hall

Kitchen

Garage

Screened porch

SECOND FLOOR

Open to below

Guest bedroom

Study/bedroom

the needs of many families today. With a master bedroom on the first floor and two smaller bedrooms on the second, it could function for a family with children or a couple who needed a sizable home office. (It was designed for the latter.) The kitchen, dining room, screened porch, and living hall all share a visual connection, but closing off two pocket doors between the kitchen and dining area allows for occasional formal dining. The formal main entry and informal garage entry share a mudroom, and the current owners use both the room off the entry hall and one of the bedrooms upstairs as office spaces.

The Importance of a Strong Roof

A roof is an important visual element of any house, and the stronger it looks, the better. The roof of this house gathers its strength from the way it defines the perimeter with a sharp edge and deep shadow line. That rhythm is interrupted only by an occasional shed dormer that defines an upstairs bedroom and by the screened porch, which has its own play-fully arched roof. The roof embraces and shelters, like an umbrella, and it draws elements of the exterior together so they don't look so busy.

The chimney, which has such a prominent role to play in the living hall, anchors the house to the site. It's like the stake of a tent driven into the ground, around which the plan and roof spin.

The few dormers lift off the roof in unexpected places, punctuating the stark exterior lines while bringing in light and views and creating special spaces inside.

Reinforcing What's Important

A successful house is a composition of site, plan, and exterior, but details are also important. In this house, there are three critical details that pull everything together: stairs, chimney, and eaves.

As an extension of the site, the entry hall and its staircase needed to be inviting, with just the right amount of detail to give a first impression of the quality of the entire interior. It's from the hall that you can see in both directions, back toward the site from where you came and out toward where you are going to the living hall. The combination of light-colored limestone flooring and the delicacy of the birch stair parts helps reinforce that flow from one end of the house to the other.

The graceful, light quality of the stair parts, made of birch and painted balusters, is a deliberate effort to "float" the staircase in the hall.

The stucco chimney topped by clay pots imparts a sense of mass, staking the lighter, tentlike house to the site.

Rafters and fascia boards are absent from the eaves, giving the roof a knife-like edge. Continuous venting strips along the soffit form a seamless transition between the house and roof.

As you pass through the hall, you can certainly notice and enjoy the staircase but it's not shouting at you.

The chimney makes a stronger statement. It's heavier and more massive, making it a visual anchor not only for the living hall but also for the other rooms around it. The stucco surface of the chimney breast and fireplace help add to its apparent mass, resulting in an impressive and substantial design element that is both a focus and a counterbalance to the high ceilings of the living hall. Stone would have had a similar effect, but it was beyond the budget and the stucco works just fine. The bluestone hearth is a nice compromise.

The roof eaves are a small detail, and an easy one to overlook, but they have a big impact here. When a house sports a lot of exterior trim—belt coursing, water table, large window and door casings, gutters—a beefy eaves with heavy fascia and built-up moldings works. Here the goal was to downplay the trim, to keep the exterior sleek and subtle. The crisp knife edge almost disappears, reducing the exterior to a few graphic elements appropriate for the summit of a hill. Even a detail as small as the shape of the eaves can help reinforce the house as belonging to the site, which was the goal from the outset, when the site was still covered with brush and saplings.

3

Expressing the way you live

If Mt. Vesuvius were to erupt in a typical suburban neighborhood, freezing it in time, what might people say about the houses 1,000 years from now? For one thing, they might wonder why so many of the houses faced the road. Was the view of cars going by that exciting, they might reasonably ask? Future archaeologists would also ponder the floor plans, trying to figure out how people lived back then. And what might they find? Probably a generous living and dining room, which would lead them to the conclusion that we did a lot of formal entertaining (they'd be off by about 50 years). The family room would be a complete puzzle. Was it for eating? Preparing meals? Entertaining? All three? And if so, why did these houses also have dining and living rooms? Probably the only room that would make perfect sense would be the garage, considering how tethered suburban lives are to the automobile.

I think most people scouring the suburbs for a home or a plot of land would agree that today's crop of new houses seldom

In today's floor plan, a formal dining area might still have its own space while an informal dining area might be more intimately connected to the kitchen.

Today's crop of new houses seldom reflects the way people live.

Outside terrace and inside living area combine into one free-flowing space.

reflects the way people live. (This isn't a problem just in the suburbs, but suburban houses tend to be the most common type of home being built these days.) This divorce from daily life (again, with the exception of the garage) is ironic considering that the floor plans of old houses seem much more fitting, more "intuitive." Why? Because those houses *did* reflect daily life, or at least more so than today's stock plans. The resilience of historic homes to change with the times offers us hope. It means that if we take into account the way people actually live (as well as the site on which the house sits) we can achieve something timeless, too.

A New Way of Thinking

The path to a functional, intuitive, and timeless floor plan requires a break from the conventional thinking that all houses *need* certain rooms, or even that rooms should have traditional names (many of which no longer have much relevance). If you're about to puzzle your way through a floor plan for a new house or a major addition, take a step backward and ask yourself some qualitative questions first. Where do you spend most of your time? If you could have only a few rooms in your house, which ones would they be? What are the ideal qualities of the rooms that are most important to you? When I work with couples, I ask both of them these questions separately. If there are older children in the household, I talk with them, too. The answers are always telling and open up entirely new ways of thinking that may not have come out had I asked, "Where do you want to put the living room?"

The best floor plans start with this line of thinking, and while the result can be achieved in different ways, only after describing the qualities of your dream house can you create a plan that truly expresses the way you want to live. I may pine for a private sitting room where I can read a newspaper or book separated from the rest of the house or a bustling kitchen that allows family members to take part in many important daily activities, all in one big room.

The questions will soon get more difficult. Dreaming about spaces is all well and good, but at some point a builder will need an accurate description of room sizes and placement to start fram-

This informal nook **shares light and views with a more public living area. Its private quality is enhanced by the contrast with the adjacent space, and yet the spaces remain connected.**

TIMELESS DESIGN IS ROOTED IN THE PRESENT

Timeless design transcends a particular style or fashion, but a thoughtful and distinctive floor plan will reflect the time in which it was created. Lifestyles today are more informal. Families are busier, meals are quicker, people take more work home and have more options for entertainment. The kitchen is no longer a hidden workshop but an area to entertain visitors and friends. Stately dining rooms are seldom used, even for entertaining. Our house plans should reflect these changes in our lifestyle and evolve with them in a sensible, methodical way. Only by paying close attention to these details of our lives is it possible to create something that will last into the future.

Combining a kitchen **with a screen porch, sitting area, and play space creates a new kind of living area, one that doesn't yet have a name.**

NAMING ROOMS

Rather than thinking about rooms in a
conventional way (kitchen, living room,
bedroom), a more useful approach is to
think of them in functional terms (public,
private, formal, informal).

TRADITIONAL

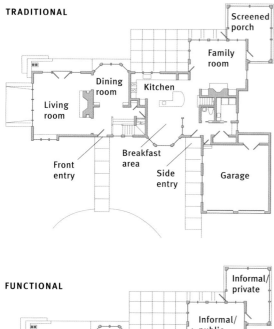

FUNCTIONAL

ing walls, floors, and roof. Stringing together rooms—and creating
hallways, doors, and windows—means adding and subtracting,
pushing and pulling until there is a comfortable fit. This chapter
describes the process most designers use to get there, but process
alone will not produce a distinctive plan. Like all elements of a distinctive house, a good floor plan is the result of seeing it as just
one more element in an integrated approach to site, plan, exterior,
and details.

By combining these two rooms into one large space, both dining room and sitting area become more informal spaces. The way the owners use these spaces would be quite different had they been designed as separate rooms.

Private or Public, Formal or Informal

Most people come up with a floor plan by listing the rooms they think they need and then laying them out in an appropriate (and usually conventional) way—the kitchen goes here, the dining room here, and so on. But I've found that a more fruitful approach is to first think of the spaces of a house in more universal terms. Rooms tend to fall into two broad categories: public/private and formal/ informal. When I think about a floor plan, my first impulse is to qualify the spaces along these lines. Is it an intimate room mainly for family and friends or will it be used (or at least seen) by just about anyone who comes over? Is there a need to transmit a stately, museum-like quality (such as a formal living room) or is it a room that won't seem unkempt with a laundry basket or a cluttered desk?

This approach may lead to more inspired spaces. For instance, rooms near a front door tend to be both public and formal. This is where guests (as opposed to close friends) enter the house. On the other hand, today's lifestyles are more informal, so perhaps this space recognizes that by being informal as well—maybe it's more open than a typical entry hall—and yet it can still be a "public" space. Typically, a formal entry would be more obvious from the street or sidewalk, fancier and more cere-monious both inside and out. An informal entry would be more discreet, its presence not so obvious. By thinking about the spaces in this way, you can make sure your intentions are reflected in your floor plan.

This isn't the easiest thing to do. Room names—living room, family room, kitchen, bedroom—are ingrained in us from child-hood, and it takes a great deal of imagina-tion to think otherwise. And in some cases, even categorizing rooms as public vs. pri-vate and formal vs. informal will lead to tra-

Formal rooms don't have to be isolated from the rest of the house. In this floor plan, the formal/public living room (fore-ground) is visually connected with a more intimate sitting area with lower ceilings and smaller proportions.

The way we combine activities that were traditionally relegated to separate rooms (kitchen, dining, and living rooms) argues for a new kind of informal, public space. This space, off a kitchen area, has a private window seat at the edge of a more public meeting area around the hearth.

Traditional room names don't do a good job of defining how the rooms will be used.

Privacy can be had just about anywhere and not necessarily indoors. This shower is detached from the house, which gives it its own magical quality.

ditional types of rooms. Kitchens are usually public and bedrooms are private. There's no getting around that. But living rooms and family rooms could go either way, and traditional names don't do a good job of defining how the rooms will be used. In fact, any room can be private or public, formal or informal no matter what activity is meant to take place there. There's nothing wrong with conventional names, but they don't necessarily get to the true ingredients that make a successful floor plan. The critical ingredients are as follows:

- Each room in the plan should be a place you really want to use. It should be functional—the right size and features— and pleasant to be in.

- Rooms need to work together. It does no good to have a great kitchen if it doesn't have convenient access to and from other related rooms.

- The floor plan should relate to the site outside. Views and sunlight are critical elements of any room. They shouldn't be ignored.

- The plan should reflect a home's exterior, and vice versa. Elements like windows and doors affect the outside as well as the inside.

- A good floor plan has interesting and well-crafted details that help define the functions and qualities of the rooms.

THE INFORMAL/PUBLIC KITCHEN

Describing rooms as public or private, formal or informal is also a way to tease out the fundamental qualities of those spaces, which in turn helps determine how big they should be, what features they should have, and where in the floor plan they ought to go. For example, until the second half of the twentieth century, the kitchen was a private, functional space and floor plans reflected that. But cleaner appliances and a move away from formality (among other societal changes) meant that a family could actually spend time in the kitchen. Floor plans changed, and gradually kitchens acquired room for a small table or sit-in bay.

Today's busy lifestyles have pushed the kitchen even farther into the center of the home. Preparing meals is now a family activity. In fact, it's one of the few times families actually get together. This, plus a growing informality in our lifestyles, led to a new kind of public and informal space: the live-in kitchen. Compared to kitchens from 100 years ago, it really isn't the same room at all. In some ways it repeats, 200 years later, the keeping room of the eighteenth-century Cape Codder, in which

Kitchens don't have to be separate, **distinct spaces. Today's activities call for a more public, informal kitchen that might visually connect both formal and informal dining with design elements such as see-through shelving and pass-through counters.**

A PLAN FOR OUR TIME

The size of new houses keeps growing, yet people still feel they don't have enough room or that the spaces they've got don't seem to work well. But the problem is really not about size but rather about the quality of the spaces.

I've often thought that a 1,200-sq.-ft., two-story house would be perfect for many people if the spaces were divided up just right. It could contain a public, informal kitchen/sitting area at one end, a small private getaway space at the other (separated by a fireplace, perhaps), with two small bedrooms on the second floor. This would be an ideal plan for our time. We spend most of our waking hours in the kitchen, but we still need at least one private room (not including bedrooms). The kitchen (or "living hall," as I would call it) would provide

both a place for meals and for informal entertaining, and the private space at the other end of the first floor might be called a withdrawing room—a place for private activities, such as watching television, listening to music, or reading. The first-floor get-away space might even double as a master bedroom or guest room. This arrangement could work well for a couple or even a small family.

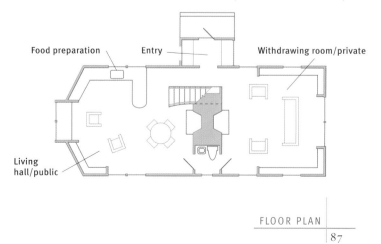

Food preparation   Entry   Withdrawing room/private

Living hall/public

The principal living space in this house includes the kitchen, dining area, and sitting area, forming a multipurpose room that's both public and informal. The informal quality is reinforced by the fir plywood box to the right, which contains a linen closet, powder room, display cabinet, and stereo equipment.

CAPE COD PLAN

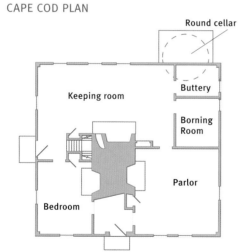

The first floor of the eighteenth-century Cape Cod house contained a simple arrangement of spaces: the keeping room (an informal/public space), a parlor (a formal/public space, which sometimes doubled as a master bedroom, private space), and a small bedroom. The informality and multifunctional quality of the spaces are a good model for today's living patterns.

most of the daily activity occurred around a fireplace used both for cooking and warmth. Why then continue to call such a room a kitchen? It doesn't really describe how this new room is actually used in our daily lives.

The same is true for the ubiquitous family room, that relatively recent invention that no one can describe with any accuracy or universality. When I was growing up, the notion of a family room didn't exist. But as radio, television, and electronic home entertainment gradually took over our leisure time, the family room began to gain prominence over the traditional living room, which became the most formal (and most seldom used) room in the house.

The reality today is that the live-in kitchen and the family room have become one space. And terms like *live-in kitchen* don't adequately describe these spaces anymore. A few years ago, I began to call this new space a "living hall" because it seemed to describe well an informal/public space that was used for cooking, dining, and living.

You may have your own ideas about new room names. Houses need functional spaces, but how these spaces are used changes over time, and there certainly will be future functions never before imagined. Don't just think about the way you actually use rooms but also think in general terms—private or public, formal or informal.

Rooms and relationships

Imagining unbuilt rooms is hard enough, but you can't think about rooms in isolation. A floor plan must be more than a series of rooms if it's going to create spaces that make sense. Rooms need to reflect not just daily activities but their *relationship* to one another. For instance, you wouldn't put a quiet study next to an eat-in kitchen with cathedral ceilings. The spillover of noise, foot traffic, and general bustle would render the quiet space all but useless. Instead, a quiet space would be better tucked off in a corner, near bedrooms and away from hubs of activity. Relationships like these—between private and public, formal and informal as well as among activities such as cooking, entertaining, eating, sleeping, and reading—serve as the glue that holds the floor plan together. It's hard to create a successful room with actual dimensions and features without understanding these relationships first.

In some ways, the relationships among rooms are more important than the rooms themselves. Rooms or spaces inside a house can have different relationships, expressed by their position and how they are connected. Imagine a corridor with a kitchen at one

Transition Zones

In architecture, a transition zone usually connects two distinct areas or spaces. Transition zones are usually defined by a physical quality, one that differs from the adjacent areas it is meant to separate. A hallway is an example of a transition zone—it can be narrow or wide, darker or lighter, or step up or down.

Transition zones can connect public spaces (like a front walk) to private areas (like a backyard). A pergola-covered entry connecting a garage and house, a bridge connecting two spaces, or even an exterior entry porch are examples of transition zones. In outdoor spaces, transition zones can be exposed or fully protected from the weather, they can be enclosed behind fencing or walls or be wide open, they can produce the appearance of separation through different materials or colors, or they can be higher or lower than the adjacent areas. Transitions also offer opportunities for whimsical elements and to enhance the experience of visitors as they approach from the street or a driveway.

Sometimes the alternative **to more rooms is having a few informal, private areas to get away to. The columns and other natural detailing, including stone and stucco, add to the informal character of these outdoor spaces.**

A Perfect Union

By borrowing features of a traditional New England barn with free-flowing interior spaces, Hillside House is a perfect blend of new and old, both in its exterior and its floor plan. Set in a pine forest, this 2,400-sq.-ft. house has a wonderful sense of openness inside and out—a great example of combining a condensed with a comprehensive floor plan (see pp. 102–107). The kitchen, bedrooms, bathrooms, and playroom loft form a tightly organized core, while the living, dining, and music areas are organized into a single, informal, and free-flowing space.

The contrast between small rooms and large open spaces couldn't be more clearly expressed on the exterior of the house. Big expanses of glass follow the living area, while smaller, more conventional windows signify the more traditional features of the main section of the house. Outdoor decks, garden spaces, and views to the forest are natural extensions of the interior living spaces. Natural finishes and exposed structural woodwork strengthen the bond between new and old and seem perfectly fitting on this wooded site.

Large expanses of glass mark the living area, while smaller windows define the bedrooms.

FIRST FLOOR

The open areas between the entry, sitting and music area, dining area, kitchen, and even master bedroom suite (with no door!) give this first-floor plan an informal/public quality. The tightly organized second-floor bedrooms and playroom loft are more private and more traditionally set apart from each other.

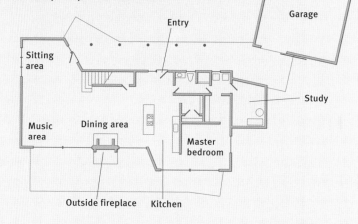

Garage

Entry

Sitting area

Study

Music area

Dining area

Master bedroom

Outside fireplace   Kitchen

Big, open rooms need to have borders, or at least landmarks, to control the space. The free-flowing, interconnected areas on the first floor are anchored on one side by the stairway to the second floor and on the other by a prominent fireplace that serves both the inside spaces and outside deck.

Public and private spaces can merge together without losing their defining qualities. The stair and balcony serve as a transition between children's bedrooms (private) without cutting them off from the informal public spaces below.

Natural finishes are combined with colorful stains to create a kitchen that is well integrated into the other details of the house. Note that there is no door between the kitchen and master bedroom, adding additional southern light to both spaces (at the expense of some privacy, of course).

The relationship between inside and outside is a key element of any good house plan.

end and a dining room at the other. The corridor takes on certain qualities because of the activities between those two rooms. Now instead of a typical corridor—a long narrow space with doors— imagine a wide space with plenty of light and perhaps an area for a desk or bookshelves. All of a sudden the corridor takes on new life: It has become a kind of hall and is now part of the connecting tissue between two spaces, with very different uses and qualities.

Every room in a floor plan should have this kind of connecting element. Even a simple door between two spaces should signify— through its size, detail, or the kind of door—something about the transition from one room to the other. These relationships can be subjective, but they are also important if your plan is going to be more than just a collection of rooms.

Marrying the Plan to the Site

Rooms and their relationships to one another clearly are important considerations, but to think of a floor plan strictly in terms of interior spaces would be to miss an enormous opportunity to use the potential of the site. A house may face toward the sun or have a good view, but it would make no sense if the only room that faced that direction was the garage. Likewise, a house may have a good floor plan that makes sense on the inside, but if it sits awkwardly on a steep site with no easy access to the outside, it won't work. A house facing south toward a good view should have a plan whose major living spaces face that direction with lots of windows, and a house sitting on a steep site should have a floor plan that meets the hill in a sensible way and takes advantage of the views that a steep site offers.

This relationship between inside and outside is a key element of any good house plan. And while it may seem obvious, it remains one of the most overlooked opportunities. It's not surprising that many homes don't feel as if they belong to their site at all. Most houses built today *can't* take into account the outside—the plans are drawn in an office and sold in a lumberyard.

The marriage of site and plan is supported in the living hall of this house by using board-and-batten siding (normally reserved for the exterior) on the wall and a barnlike window into the screened porch.

An exterior elevation should let you read something about the importance and variety of rooms in the floor plan. Here, the prominent central living hall is reflected in the high vertical window in the center, whereas the kitchen bay and bedroom windows are smaller.

Once you enter a house like this and close the door, you have no sense of where you are—it's as though you were shut out of the site entirely. A distinctive floor plan does the opposite. It brings the outside in. It embraces the site. As you develop your floor plan, always balance it with your site plan, working back and forth between the two.

THE PLAN ON ITS SIDE

We'll take a closer look at exteriors in the next chapter, but it's worth mentioning here that a distinctive plan will show itself on the exterior. In some ways, to look at a floor plan is to know the exterior elevation, and to look at an exterior is to know the plan within. The exterior elevation, in other words, ought to resemble the floor plan turned up on its side.

What do I mean? Well, I don't mean you literally turn the floor plan on its side to design the exterior walls. It's more conceptual than that. Take the floor plan of your home and, in your mind, turn it from horizontal to vertical. Then match the exterior elevation with the turned-up plan. The two should make sense together. Larger rooms should have larger windows (or more of

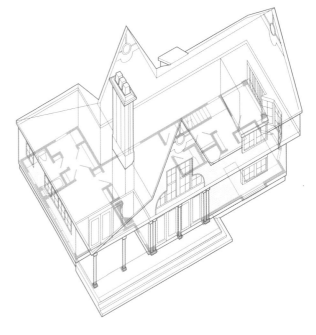

TURNING THE PLAN ON EDGE

Turning the horizontal plane up onto a vertical plane should indicate the direct relationship between plan and exterior elevation. In a distinctive house, windows, siding, and other exterior elements express the nature of the spaces within.

A Marriage of Site and Plan

Linked by sheltered walkways of steel, wood, and glass and a cantilevered pergola, this compound plan (see p. 110) creates a three-sided courtyard overlooking a valley to the south. In addition to creating new outdoor spaces, a compound plan—whether the buildings are linked or completely separate—allows for independent living areas.

In this case, the first floor of the main building consists of an informal kitchen, dining room, and study, as well as a separate, formal living room. The rooms are laid out so that each has a view and direct access to the outside. The living room is three steps down with full-height glass on three sides that can be opened to create an indoor–outdoor space. A master bedroom suite is on the second floor. The second building, which encloses the west side of the courtyard, consists of two guest bedrooms. A stand-alone carport completes the composition.

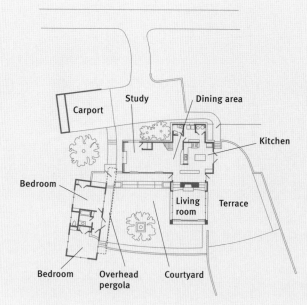

A distinctive floor plan uses parts of the house to create a better site. The two main buildings create a courtyard and shield the carport and street, opening up an interesting transitional zone for entry points. The position of the buildings takes advantage of outdoor terraces and views.

A raised outdoor courtyard and continuous pergola tie the various sections of the house together, providing a central reference point for all the rooms in the house. Turning the house inward in this way makes the private courtyard and terrace the focus, not the public driveway or carport.

The transparent quality of the formal living space created by sliding glass doors and big windows, a high ceiling, and direct access to the outdoor court on one side (and a terrace on the other) helps marry this floor plan to the site.

THINKING VISUALLY:
THE BUBBLE DIAGRAM

Bubble diagrams are the simplest and easiest way to begin the design of your house. Although they may sound (and look) technical, a bubble diagram is really just a way of arranging priorities and relationships visually.

To create a bubble diagram, first make a list of all the rooms you think you might need. Then give each room a relative priority by giving it a circle corresponding in size to the importance of the room (a small circle for the den and a large circle for the kitchen, for example). Finally, connect each circle or bubble with a line that represents the important relationships among the rooms. For instance, the kitchen may have a strong relationship with a screen porch and a family room but not with a bedroom.

By changing the size of the circles, moving them around, or connecting them in different ways, you'll start to see which relationships are important to you and which will help later with more specific problems, such as where rooms should go and which belong together.

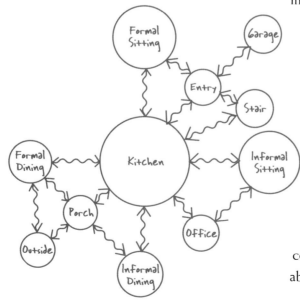

them), and smaller rooms should have smaller windows. Now imagine the larger rooms with smaller windows and the smaller rooms with larger windows. It doesn't quite make sense, does it?

Creating a floor plan that "reads" on the exterior may seem like a subtlety in the overall scheme, but what it means is that the floor plan and exterior will be integrated—the two will make sense together and the combined effect will show that logic. For instance, a room with cathedral ceilings should look like a two-story room from the outside. The windows might be taller and the exterior might have a more "open" look. It's natural that this would be the case—big windows and lots of light are part of the reason for a cathedral ceiling in the first place. The layout of a floor plan is magnified when it reads on the exterior in the form of windows, walls, and roofline. It makes sense, inside and out.

Getting Started: From Dream to Reality

It's one thing to understand what makes a successful floor plan, but how do you make it work in your own home? How do you go from dream to reality? The process has to start somewhere, and a wish list (what architects call a *program*) is as good a place as any. This can include sketches, clippings from magazines, lists of the important rooms and features of those rooms—whatever helps clarify and prioritize needs. The quality of spaces you've identified (quiet and secluded, for instance) and their relationship to one another (which spaces go together and which should be separate, for example) are best examined with sketches and diagrams.

These early drawings—sometimes referred to as *bubble diagrams*—are hardly drawings at all. Rooms are often indicated as rectangles or circles, sometimes connected by lines to indicate potential relationships. Sketches can get more complicated and detailed later on, but this is a great place to begin looking for relationships between rooms and spaces. You'll probably see a certain logic start to emerge from the bubble diagram, something about the way you live that you had not realized before.

Bubble diagrams don't say a lot about the actual plan, much less the house. Concept sketches, the next step, are the best way to

explore what might be possible. The integration of the site, the floor plan, the exterior, and the many details inside and out begins with sketches. Sketching the site plan at the same time is a good idea, and even one view of what the exterior of the house might look like. It always surprises me how close the final design of a house is to my early conceptual drawings.

Throughout the process—starting with the program and moving through the bubble diagram and sketches—I think about needs, functions, and relationships. What is the nature of each space and how do the spaces relate to each other? Will spaces be formal or informal? Is there a need to make some rooms private and others more open and public? Is this a house where many functions will be folded into a small number of large rooms, or will there be a specific room dedicated for every need as in a more traditional approach? How will the rooms relate to the site, and what will be the impact of the floor plan on the exterior, and vice-versa?

It's a deductive process. You start with the general (public or private, formal or informal) and progress to room relationships and then to specifics—real rooms with real dimensions. This isn't always how we think.

Single-story houses have a number of advantages, including fewer stairs and a larger footprint that can create a more intimate relationship to the site. One-story homes also give each room a closer look at the landscape and help bring the outdoors in.

Two-story houses are more compact and somewhat grander in scale than one-story homes. If height is a problem, it can be ameliorated by using larger windows on the first floor, or by changing the siding material on each level. Here, the narrow exterior wall along the second story makes it look shorter than it is.

SKETCHING THE FLOOR PLAN

Bubble diagrams are a good way to organize your thoughts, but you really need to see a floor plan to understand the options and possibilities. A concept sketch is different from a bubble diagram because it begins to actually define room shapes and the spaces between them. It's the first real drawing for the house, because it represents real parts of the house or positions of the house on the lot. (I always think about the site plan and floor plan simultaneously.)

Concept sketches are not exact drawings; they can be as simple as a pencil sketch on a small piece of paper. I carry a notebook with me at all times, and when I have a free moment I might sketch a particular project. The cliché of a drawing on the back of a napkin is a perfectly acceptable concept sketch. It's the first real leap toward an actual floor plan.

The direction of the stair, a series of openings, columns, and exposed beams—even the flooring direction— support the original conceptual goal of connecting the back to the front, and ultimately to the view beyond.

As indicated in the original concept drawing of this house, the architect was interested in a structured but open visual connection between the back and front of the house. The built house achieved that result by using a series of openings and columns between rooms.

EXTERIOR PLACES

LIGHT
FILTERED & BOUNCED

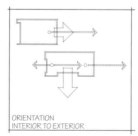

ORIENTATION
INTERIOR TO EXTERIOR

GATHERING SPACE

In the overall design process, concept sketches fall between bubble diagrams and final plans. Unlike bubble diagrams that describe relationships and only hint at size, concept sketches begin to establish actual physical shapes, accurate positioning of rooms, flow among rooms, and even volumes.

I often have clients who want to ask me detailed questions about their kitchen at our first meeting. Sure, every house will have a place to prepare meals (an important room in any house), but going right to the specifics often bypasses some interesting and exciting opportunities.

ONE STORY OR MORE?

Sketches will help answer (or at least trigger) a key question: How many stories should the house have? Sometimes the answer is easy—all the other homes in the neighborhood may be a single story, for example, or you may not want to go up and down stairs every day. Or the site may dictate two or more stories. If there is a severe slope, a single-story house will have lots of dead space surrounded by piers or columns.

Most people make up their minds early, and they most commonly opt for more than one story. It's possible that two-story houses appeal to people because of the privacy of a second floor, or it could be that one-story houses evoke the image of a somewhat unappealing ranch house. (I must admit to having this bias, probably because I grew up in the Midwest, where all I ever saw being built were one-story ranches.) But some of Frank Lloyd Wright's best houses were only one story, and so are many other fine houses. There are advantages and disadvantages to both, and a distinctive house can have one, two, or more floors—it doesn't really matter. What matters is that it fits.

Choosing how many stories usually comes down to practical considerations. One-story houses can be more expensive than equivalent two-story houses because there's more site work, foundation, and roof to build. Single-story houses are also longer (or wider), which may run into setback problems on smaller lots; but they can be more efficient in their use of space. There is less need for hallways and stairs, what architects and designers call *circulation space*. Two-story houses have their pros and cons as well. They are more compact and can be (but not always are) cheaper to build. On the other hand, some people find two-story houses inconvenient and harder to maintain.

A distinctive house can have one, two, or more floors—it doesn't really matter. What matters is that it fits.

Not all houses are pure single-story or two-story houses. Some are a mix. Combining the two has the advantage of providing a more intimate relationship to the site for the living spaces while allowing for a more compact plan.

TALL PLANS

A tall plan is a way to separate activities or to establish some boundaries between public and private spaces. It's like a compound plan, but instead of spreading functions into separate buildings, the functions are divided into separate floors. For example, placing a master bedroom on a top floor all to itself is a way to ensure privacy. Rooms for children can be far below, with the living areas in between.

Tall plans (another way to describe them is multistory plans) make sense where tall houses make sense—on steep sites. But they also work well if the building area is compact, and the only way to gain square footage is to go up. Some people just like the idea of living in a tower because there's a fanciful quality to the experience. Whatever your reasons, tall plans are unique. Of course, the inherent necessity of traveling up and down stairs may not be for everyone.

One way the architect added interest to this tall house was to add "saddlebags" to the front and back of the house. This breaks up the exterior elevation and helps alleviate one of the serious drawbacks of a tall house: that it might seem just *too* tall.

One advantage of a tall plan is the variety of light, ventilation, and view on each floor. In this case, the additional height also captures panoramic water views, while fitting right in with the soaring pine trees that surround the house.

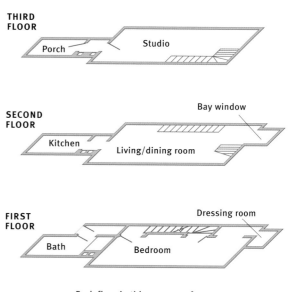

THIRD FLOOR

Porch — Studio

SECOND FLOOR

Bay window

Kitchen — Living/dining room

FIRST FLOOR

Dressing room

Bath — Bedroom

Each floor in this 1,400-sq.-ft. house is only one room wide!

The decision between a single story and multiple stories will have all sorts of implications for the look and feel of the house. Few decisions have as deep an impact. For example, one-story homes spread out more. They tend to hug the land in a more intimate way, and they can create an outside focus by enclosing a courtyard or garden, something more difficult to achieve with a two-story house. On the other hand, two-story houses can sometimes provide a better sense of separation between diverse functions, such as cooking and sleeping. There also may be more opportunities for better views from a taller house, an important consideration when tailoring a home to the site. Each has its own sense of scale that may be more appropriate for the size of the house or the context in which it is placed.

There are no hard-and-fast rules. Sometimes, it might make more sense even to combine single-story portions of the house with two-story areas. This approach may give you a better relation to the site for parts of the house while providing you with more compactness or privacy in other areas. Whatever you do, you should always consider all the options when you're designing a distinctive house.

Plan Types: Pulling It All Together

Thinking about rooms as public or private, formal or informal, understanding that those interior spaces need to respond to the site and be read on the exterior, and thinking about room relationships are critical if you want to create a distinctive home. And while it may seem that tossing convention to the wind and coming up with unique rooms is a recipe for wildly bizarre and random floor plans, the opposite actually happens. Rooms feel comfortable, their functions are clear, and their relationships to other rooms make sense. There are no dead spaces, and views actually seem to enhance the outdoor landscape.

In fact, this unconventional thinking leads to a logical result—the plan will make sense in a fundamental way. It may not be apparent, but what starts to emerge is a *type* of floor plan. By type I

A CONDENSED PLAN

This plan packs a lot of potential functions into a small space. Though certain areas of the plan are designated for specific functions and each space has its own distinct qualities, such as dining room and conservatory, one could easily imagine interchanging functions. The designated living area or the conservatory, for instance, could just as easily be a dining area on certain occasions.

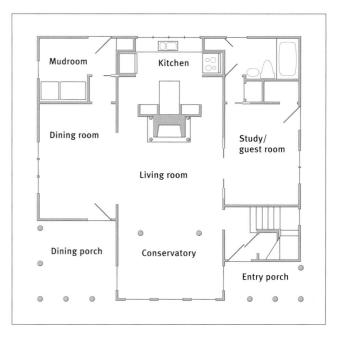

Underneath the simple hipped roof is an equally simple floor plan (shown above) in which the many different activities of daily life are condensed into a handful of rooms. The large roof overhang provides covered decks all around the house.

Small houses mean rooms need to take on different roles. Here, the story-and-a-half conservatory doubles as a dining area, and the lower ceiling demarcates a more private (but still open) sitting area. The trim over the doorway openings helps tie the rooms together, while the columns reinforce the subtle separation. (The exterior and plan of this house are shown on p. 101.)

don't mean a historical style. A four-square floor plan is certainly a type of plan, but the type of plans I'll describe have more to do with general qualities. For example, small houses have to maximize space, and this leads to a type of plan that merges lots of different functions into a small number of rooms. But larger houses can also have a condensed plan if the goal is openness and informality. Floor plan types do not necessarily refer to a specific size of house, although size will sometimes limit the type of floor plan that's possible.

A more traditional type of plan would have separate rooms for separate functions (and, I hope, they'd be named more descriptively than *living room* and *family room*). Then there's an alternative type of plan in which rooms are broken out into separate wings, separate floors, or even separate buildings. Over the years, I've identified three major types of plans that most people encounter: condensed, comprehensive, and compound.

These are simply the names I've come up; they aren't the only plan types out there, and not all plans fall into a pure type. Some plans are a mix of types. But a distinctive floor plan that works will always follow a certain logic and order—it will fall into a general category of some kind. It's the inevitable outcome of a thoughtful, integrated approach to the plan.

Looking at it another way, there are lots of homes that have fantastic spaces—vaulting rooms, breathtaking pavilions, and thoughtfully executed exteriors—and yet the experience of walking through them leaves one cold. Why? Ironically, despite the fact that many of these houses have what we might call conventional floor plans, they often belong to no type at all. There might be a living room, a family room, and a den, yet amid that vast acreage there's nowhere to sit down and quietly read a book. They don't seem to answer real needs, and they don't seem to make any sense. Distinctive houses don't suffer from this problem. Understanding floor plan types can help achieve a plan that really works.

THE CONDENSED PLAN

The simplest plan type is one in which there are lots of uses combined into a small number of rooms—what I call the *condensed plan.* These plans can often be the most interesting because they force

While it may seem that tossing convention to the wind and coming up with unique rooms is a recipe for wildly bizarre and random floor plans, the opposite actually happens.

A condensed plan **necessarily requires that functions such as living and dining can be combined into one space.**

Plenty of Room in a Tiny Space

A small cottage our firm designed for a tiny lot on Martha's Vineyard is a good example of a condensed floor plan, in which a few rooms share many roles. At 14 ft. by 22 ft. (a mere 616 sq. ft. on two floors—some garages are bigger!), it's the smallest plan we've ever designed. We didn't have a choice—the only way the owners could get this cottage to pass local zoning standards was to build it on the footprint of an early-twentieth-century garage/studio, which they were allowed to tear down. As a result, there was no way to avoid merging spaces into a condensed plan.

The first floor is a combination kitchen, living room, and dining space. It even contains a half-bath and mechanical closet underneath the stairs. The second floor is a single bedroom and bath. Both floors have access to outside—a deck off the first floor and covered porch off the second. We could have built walls between the kitchen and the living area or between the bath and the bedroom, but the result would have made all the spaces cramped. Instead, we used a kitchen island to both separate and connect the kitchen and living area. This meant that the entire first floor could take advantage of the light and views. Condensed plans can be deceptively simple from the outside, and yet still have lots of variety (and even some privacy) on the inside.

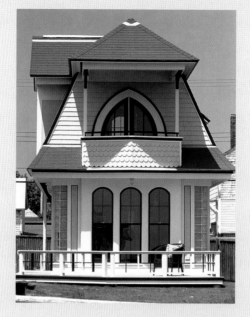

Shoehorned between two larger houses, **this small cottage defers to its neighbors** by sharing local features such as dormers, shingle siding and roofing, and light natural colors. But it also stands on its own by mixing up the rooflines differently and using alternative materials, such as the contemporary glass-block windows at the corners.

At night, the cottage glows like a lantern, which seems quite appropriate for its type and size. This kind of intimacy and openness is common for houses with condensed plans.

Because the various functions of a condensed plan are combined into one or a few spaces, the interior finishes such as ceiling or flooring materials and stair details can also be combined to create a more unified whole, or they can be used to set one area apart from another without using walls. In this case, the kitchen island serves as a boundary between living area and kitchen.

SECOND FLOOR

Bedroom

Covered porch

FIRST FLOOR

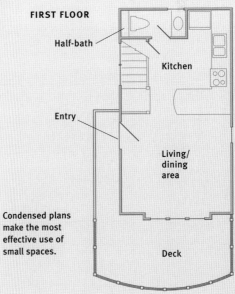

Half-bath

Kitchen

Entry

Living/ dining area

Condensed plans make the most effective use of small spaces.

Deck

The simplest plan type is one in which there are lots of uses combined into a small number of rooms.

the designer and homeowner to think of rooms in new ways. In a condensed plan, dining rooms and living rooms can share a space with a kitchen. Because there's lots of sharing going on, spaces tend to be on the informal side.

The number of people who will be living in the house is another key factor when you're looking at a condensed floor plan. There will be less privacy—fewer rooms means there won't be as many places to hide out in, or to send children to where they can make a mess (or a racket) out of sight. On the other hand, condensed plans are ideal for vacation homes and weekend retreats, or for young couples and empty-nesters. Keep in mind, though, that houses with more square feet can still have a condensed plan. The spaces may be larger but the concept of fewer rooms sharing multiple functions still holds no matter what the size.

THE COMPREHENSIVE PLAN

Openness—the strength of most condensed plans—is also its biggest weakness. Lots of big, open rooms can be difficult to control visually, acoustically, and even functionally. In a big open

A COMPREHENSIVE PLAN

A comprehensive plan typically contains a wide variety of rooms—often specifically detailed for a particular use—that allow more options for public/private, formal/informal spaces.

This is a large house with lots of rooms, reflected by the many sets of windows and dormers (floor plan at left). In a comprehensive plan, there's more opportunity for the expression of informal and formal areas, such as entries and even outside entry covers.

A large screened porch that can be used for dining (or just relaxing) connects the three separate structures of this compound plan (floor plan below).

space, it's difficult for the person cooking a meal to watch the news while someone else is listening to music or visiting with friends—the two activities interfere with each other. Condensed plans also tend to be more public and more informal, which can be a problem if you want a more stately room for displaying art or fine furniture.

The opposite approach to the open, condensed plan is the comprehensive plan, and for better or worse, most house plans fall into this category. In a comprehensive plan, rooms are basically separate. Spaces that are public or private, formal or informal are spread around the house and can be used independently of each other. By their nature, some rooms in a comprehensive plan are more important than others. Some are big, some are small, some have lots of stuff in them, others are spare. It affords the opportunity to isolate activities (working at a computer, for instance, or watching TV). On the other hand, carving up the floor plan into discreet functions chews up space, and it makes the connections between those spaces—hallways, stairs, partition walls—all the more important. Comprehensive floor plans, therefore, tend to work best in larger houses. In especially large floor plans, there may be room for highly specialized rooms, such as a library, music room, or even a guest wing.

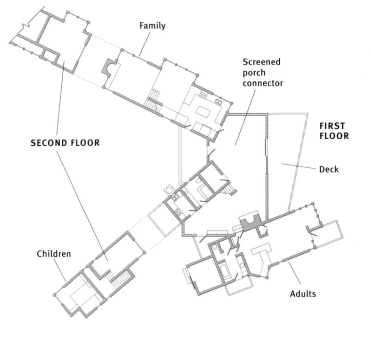

A COMPOUND PLAN

The owners of this vacation house wanted the design to support "collective and independent pursuits," and they wanted to use at least a part of the house in the off-season. A compound plan made up of independent living areas for children, adults, and family (that could be shut up separately) connected by a large screened porch enabled them to do just that.

A Hybrid Plan

Not all houses fit neatly into a single type of floor plan. Part condensed plan and part comprehensive plan, this house on Martha's Vineyard is a good example of a hybrid plan. Three large first-floor spaces in the main house are connected by parallel halls along the exterior walls. A central vaulted space serves as both an entrance hall and, on occasion, a formal dining area (perfectly illustrating how some rooms can serve many different purposes—the hallmark of the condensed plan).

By creating two wings, the central hall makes all the difference. Had that hall not been inserted into the plan, it would have been a more typical open floor plan—with the stair, bath, and fireplace separating the informal kitchen/eating area on one end from the more formal living area at the other end. The insertion of the hall not only allows guests to see through the house when entering, from front to back, but also gives each room more flexibility for use.

This main house and garage/guest house sit near the ocean amid forest, marshes, and open farmland. Wetlands setbacks limited the location and footprint of both buildings, which are tied together though a similar vocabulary of hipped roofs, arched windows, and large overhangs for protection from the weather.

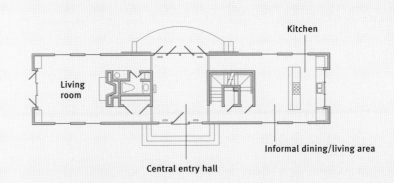

Kitchen

Living room

Central entry hall

Informal dining/living area

This simple, small hybrid plan balances the multiple-use spaces between formal and informal. The plan is just one room wide, which means plenty of light and ventilation throughout.

A central hall serves as an open entry point, connecting the house to the site. It can also be used a dining area on formal occasions.

In an open condensed plan, devices such as this high counter serve as barriers between areas (here, the kitchen and informal dining/living room). By not using a full-height wall, the architect allowed light to penetrate through the entire end of the house.

In a compound plan, similar uses or functions are brought together in one space and separated from others.

This compound plan **allowed the architect to reflect the vocabulary of a local fishing village made up of small buildings with interconnecting spaces on the exterior of this house. (The interior is shown on the facing page.)**

Just because spaces are more defined in a comprehensive plan doesn't mean some rooms won't have multiple uses. (A "pure" comprehensive plan would be a maze of rooms, and a "pure" condensed plan would resemble a barn.) There can be a condensed portion of the floor plan in a larger comprehensive plan—a wide open kitchen, sitting, and TV area would be a common example. The difference is that in a comprehensive plan, a room and its furnishings are much more likely to be defined by their primary purpose.

When does a condensed plan merge into a comprehensive one? It's hard to say, but if you add up all the basic space requirements of living, eating, bathing, and sleeping (two bedrooms), plus space for hallways and stairs, the total approaches 1,200 to 1,500 sq. ft. Anything greater than that and you're likely to start giving various functions more distinct spaces. Anything smaller and it would be hard to have many rooms and still meet code (and comfort) requirements.

THE COMPOUND PLAN

You can combine a few functions into one space or you can provide a space for each function. An entirely different approach is to separate spaces (and activities) into unique, individual locations under separate roofs. This is what I call a compound plan. In a compound, similar uses or functions are brought together in one space and separated from others. The distinguishing features of a compound plan are the connectors between the separate structures (see the photo and plan on p. 107). These can be indoors (as with an enclosed breezeway) or outdoors (as with a screened porch, deck, path, or patio). These connections open up all sorts of opportunities for tailoring the house to the site, creating new outdoors spaces, or gaining views and sun-filled areas.

There are a number of other reasons to choose a compound floor plan. Separate structures can create total privacy, say, between living rooms and bedrooms. You might want to separate a formal living area from an informal living area or to create a place for children to have a world of their own. Distributing spaces in this way provides all sorts of separations: visual, acoustic, olfactory, or even psychological.

Living, dining, kitchen, and an office share multiple levels in one of three long rectangular boxes of this compound plan (shown on p. 107). The separate buildings are detailed inside and out to fit in with the fishing shacks nearby.

One Hallway, Lots of Rooms

The central hallway that runs the length of this comprehensive floor plan is its strength. The hallway is the major artery through the main house and connects the separate studio wing. A series of doors, columns, and beams along the length of the hall act like gates that signify passage from one area of the house to another, helping integrate what could have been a jumble of small rooms with no real connection to each other.

In this plan, the kitchen, dining, and living rooms are single-loaded—they are off one side of the hall. The bedrooms are double-loaded, being off both sides of the hall at the end of the corridor. This means that access to each public room is through another room—by passing through a common door—or off the hall. And because they are tucked at the end, each bedroom has more privacy.

One of the big advantages of a single-loaded floor plan is that it keeps the house narrow along the axis of the hallway, opening up more opportunities for natural light, cross-ventilation, and a sense of the site in a number of directions.

The combination of custom windows, wood siding, and carefully detailed exterior trim gives this single-story house a comfortable fit on its site. A covered porch off the master bedroom (at right) offers another connection to the outdoors.

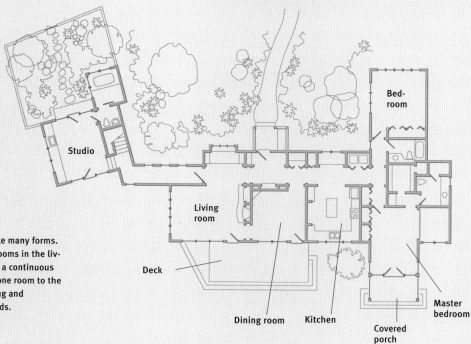

Comprehensive plans can take many forms. In this example, a series of rooms in the living wing are tied together by a continuous corridor, or a passage, from one room to the other, while the bedroom wing and attached studio are at the ends.

Studio

Bedroom

Living room

Deck

Dining room   Kitchen   Master bedroom

Covered porch

Nooks, columns, beams, doors, and even a house "altar" break up the interior space without carving it up into separate rooms. Walking through the central hallway is akin to passing through a series of gates, and each area is exposed to the outdoors.

A two-story studio, added on after the original house was built, is connected to the main house by extending the central hall. Vertical board-and-batten siding defines the second floor as separate from the shingled first floor.

By splitting up this house into a compound of three separate buildings, the architect was able to make the size of the buildings more appropriate to the landscape. It also opened up a new siting opportunity—the low, stone wall that connects the buildings and joins the whole compound to the site.

One of the best ways to add variety in any house is to change not only the room dimensions but also their heights.

This part of the compound is just one room deep, which means plenty of ventilation, abundant light, and panoramic views to the fields and water beyond.

There are downsides to compound plans. Moving from one area of the house to the other over longer distances can be a major inconvenience. There's just a lot more ground to cover. There's also the expense. More buildings and connectors mean more site work and higher construction costs and can also contribute to increased heating and cooling costs (which is why compound plans are much more common in mild climates and for summer homes).

The benefits of a compound plan can be enormous. First there are siting advantages. The individual buildings can spread over a lot like beads on a string, carving out views and exterior spaces that capture the sun in unique ways. Compound plans also open up an opportunity to reduce a home's mass. There's more detail about massing and scale in the next chapter, but a compound plan allows you to take a big, massive building and break it down into smaller pieces, which tends to be more intimate and sensitive to the surrounding landscape. (This is one way to overcome the

common problem of building a house that's just too big for its lot or neighborhood.)

Another advantage, though less obvious, is the ability to inject more variety into each room. A typical house usually can't have a two-story space in the living room because there are bedrooms upstairs. In a compound plan, the bedrooms may be in a separate building, making a one-and-a-half- or two-story space possible. One of the best ways to add variety in any house is to change not only the room dimensions but also their heights. Compound plans make that easier than most other plan types.

THE SYSTEMATIC PLAN

Before leaving the subject of floor plans, there's one more type worthy of mention: the systematic plan. Most people design a house around their need for space, comfort and pleasure, recreation, entertainment, and even spectacular views. The important thread is that the design *follows* the need. The order comes after—not before—determining the functions. But there's another way to go. You can create a preexisting order for the floor plan and fit the

A simple stone path, which almost seems to be older than the house, and a few trees establish a circulation path in the courtyard between the studio and the house.

Indoors Meets Out

Compound plans solve the problem of creating houses that are too big for their
sites. Rather than put all that space under one
roof, a compound floor plan allows you to
spread the rooms out over two or more separate (or loosely joined) buildings, each on a
smaller scale. It also creates opportunities
for forging new outdoor spaces between the
buildings—for courtyards, private patios, or a
more interesting entry point.

This compound on Martha's Vineyard
includes a main house, barn, and guesthouse
as well as a pool and spa. All of the buildings
share a barn-like vocabulary (in keeping with
the historical quality of the island architecture).
Stone terraces and paths, arbors, gardens,
stone walls, and grass paths in a meadow act
as transition zones among the various buildings in the compound, while creating a number
of interesting outdoor spaces.

Open and informal, the
guest house floor plan
is a hybrid—a con-
densed plan within a
compound. Living, din-
ing, and kitchen are
essentially a single
space under one roof.

At first glance, the arrangement of
the various buildings seems arbitrary, but a closer look reveals that
there are subtle alignments that
create new outdoor spaces.

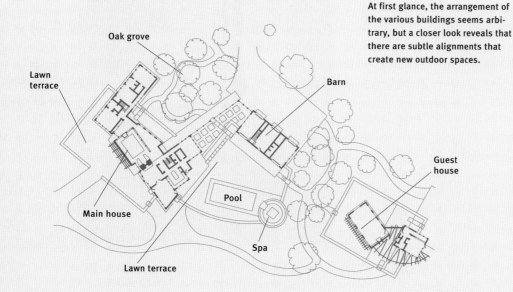

Oak grove

Lawn
terrace

Barn

Main house

Pool

Spa

Lawn terrace

Guest
house

Stone paths and walls, arbors, and a mowed grassy path through a meadow are used to tie the various buildings of the compound together.

By breaking down the various components of the main house into formal living; informal living, dining, and kitchen; and private sleeping, the architect was able to give each component a smaller scale than would have been possible under one roof.

The pattern of the columns, glass, and laminated-wood trusses sets the stage for the floor plan (shown on the facing page). This is the signature of the systematic plan, in which the underlying order is established first, and the rooms are designed later to fit the system.

rooms into it. The order (or the system) can take the form of a grid, a pattern, or some other preordained system into which all the rooms will fall.

This somewhat rigid, systematic approach may seem like a strange way to design a house, but some designers prefer it. Late in his career, Frank Lloyd Wright used triangles, hexagons, and circles in this way. The French architect Le Corbusier established modules, tuned to human dimensions, that he proposed for the design of all buildings. Traditional Japanese houses are laid out in a grid pattern that corresponds to the size of a tatami mat, giving them their instantly recognizable uniformity.

Systematic designs can be difficult to shape into workable floor plans, especially in the later stages of the process when specific dimensional requirements may not coincide with the predetermined system. But they have some advantages. Ideally, the order and clarity of the system will show itself in the final product as sublimely natural. It may even make the building process easier—a rigid system predetermines the sizes and shapes of rooms.

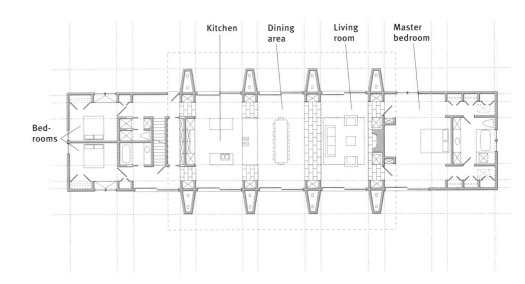

Kitchen   Dining area   Living room   Master bedroom   Bedrooms

A SYSTEMATIC PLAN

Systematic plans typically start with a preestablished order that overlays the entire plan. In this example, alternating narrow portions of the house that contain structure, niches for the homeowners' folk art collection, flooring material changes, and even plumbing fixtures are interspersed with a more traditional plan type.

Hearth as Home

This chapter illustrates that a distinctive floor plan follows from a number of factors: fulfilling functional needs, identifying room qualities, and thinking about the relationships among rooms so that they work together—whether there are lots of rooms or just a few.

But a great house also has a spiritual, even inspirational quality. I think it has something to do with the common understanding we have of a home as *hearth*. It is not necessarily the fireplace but rather that central place that stands for the essence of what a home is—a refuge, a sanctuary from the outside world, a place of comfort and security. This has deep significance, because it gets at the real nature of a successful floor plan. It speaks to all of us as a means of expressing the way we want to live in our own time. We feel instantly comfortable in homes like this. A distinctive floor plan can, at a glance, convey what is important in our lives.

A night view illustrates how compelling a preordered, systematic plan can look when its parts are expressed on the exterior.

A House Becomes a Village

DESIGNING A SUMMER
HOUSE ON AN ISLAND
with commanding ocean views
would seem like a fairly straightforward
project, especially when the house is for
your own family, as it was in this case.
But nothing is easy on the island of
Nantucket. Situated off Cape Cod,
Nantucket has delightful weather in the
summer, but for much of the rest of the
year it can be downright nasty. As a result,
much of the early architecture on this
island is tightly clustered, huddled in
response to the elements. How to create a
house that gave the family protective
comfort from the elements on the one
hand and yet was breezy and light-filled
on the other turned out to be a challenge.

History played a role, too. Local historical guidelines are stringent and can, in

SITE PLAN

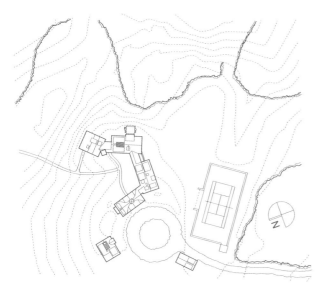

This site—isolated by the ocean and conservation land, yet conveniently close to town—made the perfect location for an island house.

The living and guest buildings of the compound surround the courtyard, which is on a bluff overlooking the Atlantic.

the wrong hands, be stifling. All the houses on the island, for example, must be painted (if they are painted at all) a particular shade of gray with white accents. (The local joke goes something like, "I'll meet you at the gray house with the white trim.") The goal for this house was to pay homage to the architectural heritage of the island while creating a unique interpretation of that history.

Starting with the Site

The homeowners spent a number of summers on the island looking around for the right piece of property before settling on this one. They wanted something that was isolated enough to have some privacy without being too far from town.

What they found was a 7-acre plot on a bluff that faced the ocean on one side, with a large tract of conservation land (once a golf course) on the other. The former golf course passed into the hands of the Nantucket Preservation Commission, which meant it would never be built on. In effect, they had purchased a kind of island within an island.

But the exposure of the site to the ocean—part of the goal of living on Nantucket—also posed a dilemma. At times they would want the house to be

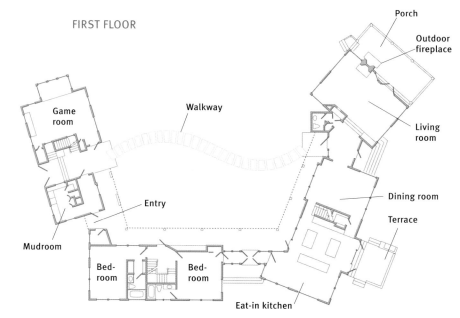

FIRST FLOOR

Porch

Outdoor fireplace

Walkway

Game room

Living room

Entry

Dining room

Mudroom

Terrace

Bed-room

Bed-room

Eat-in kitchen

A courtyard facing north to the ocean allows covered, shaded, or open sun-filled areas.

An open barn door–like breezway serves as a gate between the public world of entry and the private living world beyond.

SECOND FLOOR

Bedroom

Bedroom

Family room

Master bedroom

wide open to the view and the warm salty breezes. But at other times, they would need shelter from the gales. Fortunately, the site suggested a solution. Rather than erect a big house and steel it against the elements, why not make it a series of smaller buildings—a compound—with a courtyard facing the ocean. This would carve out a space protected from the cold northeast winds, which didn't exist before, and would not sacrifice the great ocean views and exposure to the warm south-westerly breezes of summer. And because all the interior spaces are small—only one room deep—each one has lots of light and cross-breezes.

Each building is made of the same materials; but each has a unique character, created by the windows and rooflines. The overall effect implies that the compound was built over time.

Because some first-floor spaces in this house have no rooms above them, there is a great variety of volumes. High windows let light penetrate deep into the living room.

A Village of One

The compound plan turns what might have been a single, large house (all too common in summer places these days) into a kind of village clad in weathered cedar shingles with simple trim that defer to the historical character of the other houses on the island. The barn-like shapes of all the buildings are simple and direct, and the roof is plain, except for places where there is a need for extra headroom. And unlike many seaside houses, not all the windows are huge. Their size depends on the importance and quality of the space inside, and some are quite small. The result is a microcosm of the town of Nantucket in the distance. If it weren't for

By breaking down the house into a series of smaller structures, the architect gave the compound the feeling of a historical village.

the surrounding conservation land, one can almost imagine the town growing up around the house and the house fitting right in.

The compound is composed of distinct parts connected by walkways inside and out. There is also a separate guest house and garage, which are not connected but are still part of the layout of rooms and functions. The buildings are organized around two courtyards. One is formed by the wings of the main house; the other, on the southeast side, is an entry court formed by the main house, garage, and guest house. Each building seems to lead to the other, accommodating the topography individually—another benefit of compound plans.

The four sections of the main house are connected by a covered walkway and partially enclosed breezeways that face the water. The wings appear to have evolved over time as the family has grown—not an uncommon phenomenon in New England. Arriving at the entry court, visitors get some sense of what lies

The kitchen is the heart of the compound, serving as the commons to the village of buildings.

The transparency of the single-room-wide buildings is most apparent in the evening.

Passing through a gate before entering the private realm of the house is a great way to add a layer of privacy and separation/transition from a street or driveway.

beyond, but it's not until they pass through the open breezeway that they see the spectacular vistas and the actual entrance. Passing through a kind of gate before entering the private realm of the house is a great way to add a layer of privacy and separation/transition from a street or driveway.

The main house contains a living room with an outdoor porch, dining room, eat-in kitchen, outdoor terrace, game room, upstairs family room, and a number of bedrooms on both floors. Because there are no rooms above them, both the living room and eat-in kitchen are dramatic two-story spaces. It's a comfortable plan for summer living and entertaining. You can be inside or outside, covered or out in the open, alone or together, in the sun and breeze or out of them.

The eat-in kitchen is the heart of this plan. Its ample size, good light, and interesting gull-like trusses provide an atmosphere conducive to eating, reading, relaxing, or playing no matter what the season. In a way, the kitchen is the commons of this "village."

Evocative Details

This is a house whose details, inside and out, recall many of my own childhood memories and yet, like all distinctive details, seem also to belong only to this house. The lighthouse-like tower next to

Each stair in this house has its own quality, appropriate for its use.

The whimsical but metaphorical nature of the lighthouse-like tower is a strong icon for this oceanside house.

the entry is one example. It's whimsical and doesn't actually do much except provide light into a small latticed bathroom on the first floor. But there's more to it than that. From the open breezeway it signals the entry in a metaphorical way while recalling the older lighthouses that, like this house, sat alone on bluffs overlooking the ocean. It's not real, of course, but it doesn't pretend to be.

The cedar lattice on the roof facing the courtyard (shown in the photo on pp. 120–121) is another detail that grows out of the house below. The way it mimics a dormer and provides high light to the eat-in kitchen below, through a skylight, is particularly effective. It recalls the small fishing village of Siasconset on the same island, and you can imagine how magical the courtyard becomes when flower-covered vines find their way up and around the lattice. Frank Lloyd Wright used to say that "doctors bury their mistakes and architects cover them with plants," but this is an exception.

A couple of details that are especially appealing in this house are the stairs. Each set has its own magical quality. The stairway leading to the family room is a straight run with a window at the top of the landing. It is treated with glossy white paint to reflect as much light as possible. Another stair twists and turns its way up to the guest bedrooms. Its windows are small, its walls are stained, and the rails have a storybook character.

Balancing function and beauty

I once had a client who got upset with me because I refused to give him a historical label for the house I was designing for him. The plans borrowed historical elements yet belonged to no particular style, but that didn't help. He wanted a way to describe it, and he was frustrated that I could not come up with one. I suggested that we would discover the style together as we worked our way through the design process. He finally agreed and we went on to complete a successful house, but I've never forgotten how important it was to him (and to others since then) that a home's style fall into a certain category. It's almost as if the label—such as colonial, Tudor, or contemporary—would make it seem real and understandable.

When people describe houses with these kinds of labels, what they are referring to are exterior characteristics—the particular blend of rooflines, siding, trim, windows, doors, and porches. For better or worse, these labels have stuck. People want their houses to belong to a period of history or at least to find their roots

Most people want a home that looks timeless from the outside. But how to create it? The best way is to look outward to the site and neighboring houses and inward to the floor plan. Rather than *starting* with a style, you *end up* with one.

NAMING HOUSES

I've always liked the idea of giving a house a name: *Goosewing Farm, Hemlock House,* and *The Point House* are just a few examples. Sometimes the name is simply the result of the house location (for instance, the house is on a point at the end of a road). The origin of the name is less important to me than the fact that the house has a name, because naming a house gives it a significance that raises it above the ordinary. It places the house on the site or in its historical context in a way that a straightforward post office address doesn't. There's no guarantee that the post office will deliver the mail, but you'll have given the house a distinctive characteristic.

somewhere in the past. And that's fine, because labels can be useful, but they are also limiting. If you start out with a style in mind, you'll end up with it, but often at the expense of a thoughtful and distinctive solution, one that integrates the site, the floor plan, the exterior, and the details inside and out. It makes more sense to look at all the options for integrating these critical elements and then to *end up* with a style.

This isn't easy. There are trade-offs everywhere you look, and you'll find yourself constantly weighing options, trying to balance function and aesthetics. For example, a thoughtful, functional floor plan may not always lead to the perfect roofline or window placement. The varieties and permutations that arise as you try to match inside and outside are almost endless, and the task may seem overwhelming. The process is a difficult one, and, once again, the stakes are high because a home's exterior is what people see first. It sets the tone for everything else.

Another reason house styles are limiting is because a house can have many styles, or what I prefer to call *personalities.* It can look a certain way from a distance and another way up close. Rooflines, materials, colors, chimneys, porches, entries, and trim details transmit all kinds of messages about the nature and quality of the house. Just moving some walls, changing colors, or swapping clapboards for shingles can change that personality in subtle or dramatic ways.

As with siting and floor plans, I start the design process by considering the exterior of the house in a general way. I try to imagine the house as a visitor would—from a distance. This is how we all experience a house for the first time. It's like meeting someone on the street: From a distance, a first impression might be limited to the color of a person's clothing, the length of the person's hair, or the way the person moves. But as the individual approaches, he or she becomes clearer and the details of the face and clothing are more apparent. The visual clues are moving from general to specific. The same is true of houses.

One reason house styles are limiting is because a house can have many styles or personalities.

A timeless house blends with the landscape in different ways. From the meadow, the tree frames this farmhouse to create a powerful but simple composition.

Whether humble or grand, awe inspiring or just plain welcoming, a home's first impression is made from a distance.

The House from a Distance

Whether humble or grand, awe inspiring or just plain welcoming, a home's first impression is made from a distance. A house from a distance is about big statements, not details. Scale, massing, and color are the most apparent qualities to consider from a distance, because these are the features that will stand out.

Scale refers to size: How big is the house compared to the people who live in it? Some houses have fabulously overscaled entries, with monumental columns and arches. You get a humbling, vaguely uneasy feeling when you enter a house like this. On the other extreme, some houses demur to the surrounding landscape—because of their intimate size—so much so that they almost disappear.

Similarly, a home's *massing*—its volume or bulk—has a big impact in tailoring the home to its site. We've all seen boxy houses that provide acres of space inside but seem too massive compared to the land or neighborhood around them. *Color* makes a big difference as well. The right combination of colors can make a house either stand out from the pack or blend quietly into the surrounding landscape. Considering that adding variety through color adds practically nothing to construction costs, I'm always amazed how little it is exploited as a critical element of an exterior. Taking full advantage of all three factors—scale, massing, and color—is the first step toward an integrated and distinctive exterior.

SCALE AND MASSING: WHAT'S THE DIFFERENCE?

I f a person stands next to a large object—say, an ancient pyramid—there are obvious differences of size and weight between the person and the pyramid. Each is out of scale with the other. Sometimes (as with a pyramid) this is intentional and effective. It humbles the person and makes the object more grand. But when it comes to houses, people are most comfortable in spaces that have a scale similar to their own size.

The same is true for massing. The large volume of a pyramid makes it seem heavy in comparison to a person. It's quite obviously massive. Scale is about relative size compared to a person, massing is about rel-

ative volume, and the two are very much related. Small houses tend to be relatively small in scale and massing, whereas large houses are just the opposite. When I design houses, I often find myself trying to adjust these factors in inverse proportion—to make a large house seem not so large, and to make a small house seem bigger than it is.

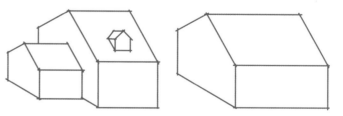

These two houses are roughly the same size and scale, but they have different massing.

Because this house sits at the crest of a hill, the umbrella-like roof appropriately serves as a man-made summit, reflected in its shape.

By their very nature, **small houses** tend to have an intimate scale with smaller room dimensions and details.

Scale and mass are key elements for large houses, because size can easily overwhelm everything else. By breaking down this exterior into base, middle, and roof and by providing an assortment of shapes, textures, and color, this large house has a human scale and pleasing mass despite its sheer size.

SCALE AND MASSING

Scale has to do with the dimensions of rooms, ceilings, doorways, and entries, the features that can make a space seem large or intimate. Cathedrals have enormous scale inside and out—soaring arches, cavernous spaces, and enormous doorways. The scale of most houses tends to be smaller than that of public buildings, but houses can range from huge mansions with massive timbers to tiny cottages. Smaller-scale houses seem more personal. There are no high walls, no sweeping archways over entry doors, and no four-car garages. Large-scale houses sometimes feel larger than life, at least in proportion to a person. For some buildings—churches, auditoriums, and ballrooms—this is intentional, but it doesn't work as well for a house.

Massing is about size, too, but it has more to do with volume—height, width, and depth—and with the shapes and proportions of those volumes. Two houses may have the same size (in square feet of floor space) and equal volume, but they may not have the same massing. For instance, the house with heavier mass might be big and boxy (like a barn), whereas a house with a lighter mass might have two smaller boxes separated by a breezeway. Generally, a house with a good scale—the right size in relation to its surroundings and occupants—will also have good massing, one that feels appropriate in bulk and weight. But it's always important to consider them both.

SCALING UP, SCALING DOWN

One of the things I often do when working on a house exterior (or interior, for that matter) is to look for ways to adjust the scale. One method for doing this is simply to make the house smaller. Cottages, cabins, and small houses usually have an intimate scale—it comes with the limited territory. Small houses like these often have a dollhouse quality that can be very appealing.

But sometimes making a house smaller just to reduce its scale is not a sensible thing to do. Floor space is precious, after all. So another way to adjust scale is to break a house down into smaller parts or even into separate buildings. This is another reason to consider a compound floor plan, as described in the previous chapter. Each section of a compound house would have a smaller scale than if all that area were combined under one roof. (Breaking a house down into parts affects massing too, but more about that later.)

Another common way to reduce the scale of a house is to keep it to a single story. Just by virtue of its height, a single-story home is more intimate in scale than a two-story house. Finally, you can reduce (or reinforce) the scale of a house through its details. Bay

These two houses are similar in size and scale but have different massing. One is is broken down into a variety of shapes, producing a lighter mass (above); whereas the other is made up of simple shapes, which results in a heavier mass (below). For each, the massing is balanced and appropriate.

Including elements such as window bays and small windows helps scale down a large house and makes it feel more compatible with our own human size.

windows, dormers, entries, columns, and brackets help bring a house down to a more human scale by inserting smaller elements among the larger features, like the walls and roof. The variety alone will temper the overall scale and make the house much more intimate and inviting. On the other hand, if entries, windows, and columns are too large or there is no variety among them, the house may seem less like a home and more like a museum.

There are times when a larger-than-life scale works. A room with a vaulted ceiling, exposed timbers, and a mountainous stone fireplace can be wonderfully comfortable as well as appropriate to the site. A number of large houses designed by McKim,

Mead & White, American architects of the late nineteenth and early twentieth centuries, are good examples. In spite of the size of these houses, I am always impressed how extraordinary the rooms are. The various parts of each room—the windows, doors, moldings, even the floor boards—all have a scale that feels appropriate. In one house, I recall that the large floor boards were turned into small parquet patterns about the size of a chair. This means that you can sit in the corner of a very large room and still feel comfortable. Remember, it's not about size, it's about good design.

Details reinforce a home's scale. **Columns, brackets, and wall and roof trim break down large elements such as roofs and walls, making them more human in size and thus more approachable and comfortable.**

GETTING THE MASSING RIGHT

A big complaint I hear these days is that many new houses are too big. But I don't think size is always the problem. Sometimes it's simply a case of ill-conceived or haphazard massing. A bulky, clunky box of a house is going to color everything else about it, from the way it sits on its site to its tiniest details. One way to consider a house exterior shape is to think of it as sculpture. You begin with a single lump of clay or stone and then you mold that lump by pushing and pulling, adding and subtracting until it takes its final form. Most new houses with bad massing are like pieces of clay that haven't yet been molded.

This doesn't mean that a single-mass house—one with basically one shape, like a barn—has to be clunky. There are many beautiful, elegant, and even sculptural barns. Old farmhouses and early American homes made up of a single box are quite handsome. But too often when these styles are copied, they seem un–appealing. Why? Because while the shapes may be similar, the proportions are all wrong—the windows are too big or too small, the roof pitch is too shallow or too steep, the porch columns are too skinny or too bulky. Unfortunately, many contemporary

Scaling a house **doesn't always mean making it look smaller. Sometimes scaling a house up so it looks larger makes sense. The two-story height of the covered porch over one section of this house is a deliberate (and successful) attempt to enlarge the scale to match the steep, wooded site.**

A Well-Scaled Compound

Getting scale and massing right is always difficult, especially with a single-mass house—one that is really just a rectangular box. It's even tougher when you have three single-mass boxes on the same property, all part of the same compound. In this case, all three buildings—main house, guest house, and boat house—have the same look and feel, although they each had different programs, or needs.

Rather than make all the buildings the same size, the architects, Van Dam and Renner, created a single-mass structure that was consistent for each building. They then achieved an appropriate sense of scale for all three by using various elements of the buildings that matched, such as dormers, chimneys, bays, materials, and color. The overall feel is of three distinct buildings that, nevertheless, seem to belong together. Their masses relate, and the scale of each is appropriate for what the building is used for.

The boat house has forms, dormers, materials, and color that connect it to the main house and to the compound as a whole.

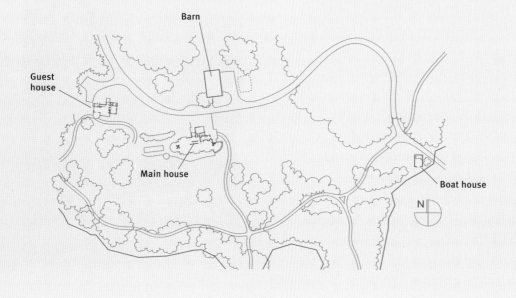

Although smaller than the main house, the guest house has compatible scale and massing because the architects broke out the dining area and bedrooms with separate wings and dormers. The arrangement of trees around the guest house is denser, giving it a more private and secluded quality.

Shed dormers for bedrooms eliminate the
need for a two-story wall except at the gable
ends, which helps lighten the massing and
create a more intimate scale.

Older farmhouses **often have simple shapes, but because they tend to be small and well proportioned, they seem to have a lighter mass. Enlarging these classic styles (as many developers do) has mixed results at best, because it changes the balance of the proportions and, therefore, the mass and scale.**

Some houses seem too large **even when they're not. The reason is not the size but the massing, which can result in a heavy, boxy, and out-of-scale building.**

American houses seem too big because *all* of these proportions are overblown, resulting in buildings that seem much more massive than they need to be.

Fortunately, massing is not that hard to adjust, which is especially important the larger the house. Single masses work best on small houses because their limited size makes it hard for them to grow too massive. But the larger the house, the larger the mass and, odds are, the heavier or bulkier it is likely to look. Breaking down one large mass into multiple smaller masses (similar to adjusting scale) is a good way to reduce the impression of bulk. This can be done by simply breaking the house into parts (using a compound plan, for instance) or by creating one large volume with smaller volumes attached (breezeways, wings, pavilions, ells, and so on).

There are lots of little ways to reduce mass as well. Projecting one story over another breaks up a single, boxy structure without complicating a floor plan. (This is a good alternative when the house footprint is limited by setbacks.) Remember, the goal is to reduce the *impression* of bulk, so using a variety of exterior wall siding—mixing up the texture and color—can have an enormous impact. Like a column, a single-mass house will seem less bulky if the base, middle, and roof all are clearly defined by different materials.

Massing can make a large house seem smaller, and, perhaps surprisingly, it can also make a small house seem large. Like scale, there is no single correct massing. But using scale and mass to your advantage is a great way to make your house more pleasing from a distance.

DESIGNING WITH COLOR

Color plays a major role in how a house looks from a distance. Color can reinforce the relationship of a home to its site, or it can set it apart. In either case, colors ought to be chosen with the environment in mind. I often take cues from the site—blending earth tones or the color of rocks and ledge, for example, if those features are prominent on the site.

The massing of this larger house was adjusted by lowering most of the roof eaves to one story, thereby making its real two-and-a-half story height less apparent. The variety of roof shapes and dormers also helps reduce its mass.

One way to improve the scale and mass of a boxlike house is to keep the forms (and details) simple and to add smaller elements such as porches, balconies, or bays.

The color of a house is not limited to its siding and trim. Dashing color in unusual places—such as the rows of contrasting shingles on the roof and the stripe running up the side of the chimney—are easy and relatively inexpensive ways to add variety and reinforce the site.

There are a variety of ways to use color. When most people think about house color, they think about the paint on walls and trim. But color extends to all elements of a house, from its foundation to its roof, and everything in between. And there's no reason to limit yourself to single solid colors. One of the most underused canvases for house color is the roof; there are plenty of roofing materials that come in colors other than gray and black. In fact, a roof does not need to be a single color at all. Why not add a pattern or stripe? I wouldn't do this on every house, but sometimes it can tie the rest of the exterior together.

If your house is close to others, you'll probably want to choose colors that fit in with the neighbors. On the other hand, colors can complement rather than match the surroundings. It's worth

In summer and fall, this white house with its Shaker-like starkness stands out brilliantly against the grass and trees. In winter, the color blends with the snow, almost making it disappear. White is not the only color this house could have been painted, but the effect is dramatic.

keeping in mind that in dense urban or suburban settings, a single house is just part of a larger composition—the street—which ought to be taken into consideration. Seasons are also important. The color that looked perfect in spring may look entirely out of place during winter, which means the choice is that much harder (unless you want to paint your house several times a year!).

The House Close Up

Not all houses are visible from a distance, but every house, ultimately, is seen up close. While the factors that influence first impressions from a distance—scale, massing, and color—are important, other qualities of the exterior begin to occupy a greater role as you get closer. It may be something about the size and placement of windows and doors or an inviting porch that begins to reveal a home's secrets. It could be something more subtle—the texture of the siding, an unexpected jog in a wall, a chimney detail. In a distinctive house none of these exterior elements is arbitrary. They all are pieces of the larger puzzle.

WALLS AND OPENINGS

Before thinking about the specific elements of the house that make a big difference close up, it's important to consider the more general issue of wall versus opening. Although it's easy to look right past them, walls are the most prominent feature of any house. Exterior walls aren't just flat surfaces that keep the wind and rain out, punctuated here and there by windows and doors; they are opportunities to build a composition of parts. Wall openings include windows and doors, but also porches, entries, and recessed areas—anything that penetrates or recedes from the flat surface of the exterior wall. The thoughtful placement of these openings can transform an exterior in remarkable ways.

A house reveals itself first from a distance **and then more and more as you get closer. A well-detailed entry—with a hint of what's beyond—is an important part of this first impression.**

The thoughtful placement of wall openings can transform an exterior in remarkable ways.

Windows and doors make more of an exterior impression when they reveal something about what's happening in the floor plan. Here, the windows show us the stair and a two-story space within.

In the Pacific Northwest, where the climate is mild and bright light is at a premium, the amount of window can greatly surpass the amount of wall. In a different climate, this arrangement would result in high heating or cooling costs.

A good way to begin thinking about exterior walls is in terms of the contrast between *solid* and *void*. Solid areas enclose, create privacy, and hide what's on the other side. Openings do the opposite. While a distinctive exterior is the direct result of siting outside and the plan within, it's also an independent composition that should have a pleasing balance of solids and voids—rather than a hodgepodge of openings that have no order. There is never just a single solution to balancing the solids and voids of exterior walls. The windows alone can range from single openings in a large amount of wall to a large amount of windows in very little wall.

Because each side of a house faces a different part of the site (and has different activity going on inside), it makes sense that each wall (or elevation) should look different. At the same time, no elevation is truly its own composition. It needs to tie into the adjacent walls somehow. When I'm designing a house, I look at all the influences of the site and floor plan on each elevation, but I also place them side by side to see how each wall relates to an adjacent elevation (see the photos and drawings on the facing page).

Two adjacent sides of a house will never be seen alone; they need to work together. Every house should feel like a whole, which sometimes means changing the size or placement of windows, doors, porches and other solids and voids. The same balancing act that takes place in looking at one wall must also occur when you're looking at all the walls together. It might be as simple as using the same or similar types of windows on each wall and using similar amounts of solid wall. Or you might choose to tie all your walls together with the same material (a common approach) or use a variety of trim pieces, as we'll discuss later. As with each wall, there is no one solution.

SOUTH SIDE

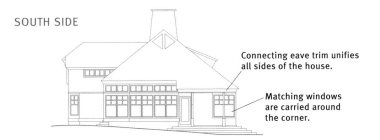

Connecting eave trim unifies all sides of the house.

Matching windows are carried around the corner.

EAST SIDE

Corner porch ties the two walls together.

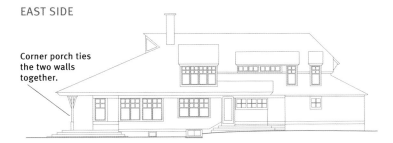

Individual walls need to work alone but also with the wall around the corner. Here, the use of similar windows, materials, and connecting trim and a corner porch ties the two walls together.

Walls and Openings: Finding a Balance

This cabin is made up of two distinct asphalt-shingle-covered wings—which contain kitchen, baths, bedrooms, and a study—bridged by a two-story living/dining space that seems to float in the middle. The central space has a tall window wall that faces north and, with the exception of windows top and bottom, a largely solid wall facing south. This runs contrary to the idea that important windows ought to face south. But in this case, there's a reason.

The owner commissioned an artwork—a sun drawing by artist Janet Saad Cook—that projects reflected images of light onto the interior of the south-facing wall. The image changes with the movement of the sun and clouds—an ephemeral response to place, time, and architecture. The exterior appears to be split down the middle and pulled apart to accommodate the work of art. Given the owners' special requirements, the balance here between window and wall seems just right.

High windows on the south-facing wall allow just enough sun to activate the sun-drawing artwork. Windows below elevate the projection wall off the floor, creating a movie-screen quality.

A high, central living/dining space literally and figuratively bridges the gap between the bedroom and study wings. The amount of north-facing glass at the center is a response both to the living area within and to the need to illuminate the artwork projections of the interior south wall.

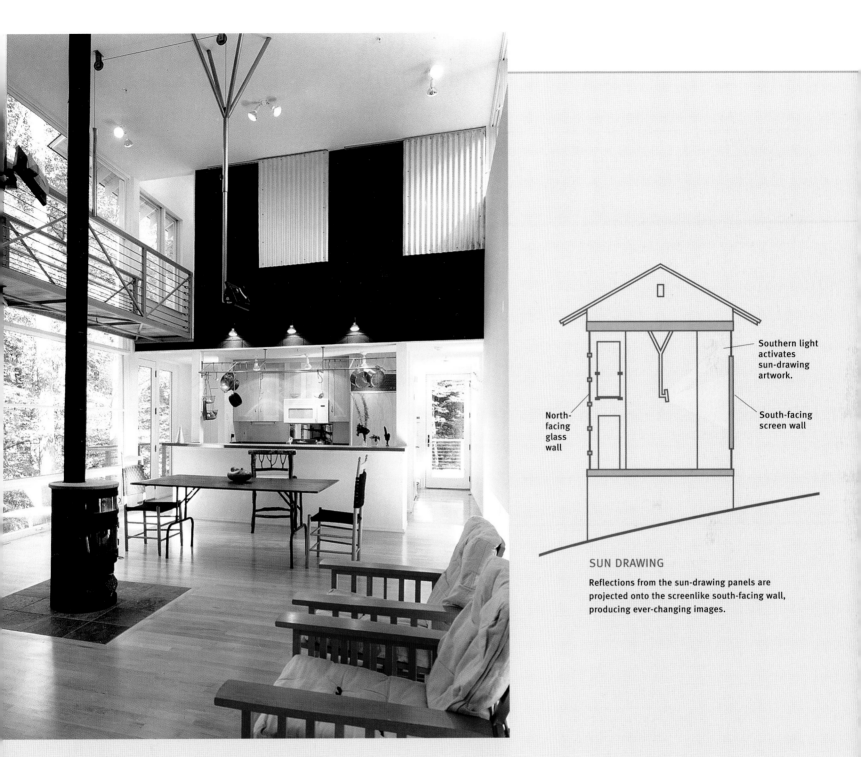

SUN DRAWING

Reflections from the sun-drawing panels are projected onto the screenlike south-facing wall, producing ever-changing images.

Southern light activates sun-drawing artwork.

North-facing glass wall

South-facing screen wall

The connecting nature of the high central space is reinforced by the light steel bridge that joins the two outer wings. Translucent panels on the upper walls allow light into the study.

Windows are the eyes of a house. **They open to the world outside and tell us something about the world within.**

WINDOWS: THE EYES OF THE HOUSE

Windows are the eyes of the house, opening up to the world outside. They also represent a large portion of the construction budget (10 percent or more), so their quality—both aesthetically and practically—says much about the care put into the house. And never before has there been as much choice in quality, style, and mechanics, which makes any decision about these critical elements all the more difficult. One way to make it easier is (as always) to

Windows are like big picture frames, **cropping views in powerful ways, depending on their placement. Here, the windows provide each diner with his or her own view of the woods, while the combination of all the windows forms a large mural.**

This novel, unexpected window **not only makes climbing the stairs a whimsical experience but also washes light over the landing, always a difficult area to illuminate.**

start with the key elements. Siting and floor plan considerations help determine the relative size and perhaps even the type of windows and doors you choose. The logic of the exterior composition will certainly help in choosing styles and settling on placement.

For example, a small house with a good view in one direction would probably call for smaller windows on three sides with a larger window (or more windows) in the room facing the view. It might also make sense to add multiple mullions to give the windows a smaller scale, consistent with the size of the house. The

The type and size of the windows should be consistent with the exterior siding and trim.

Windows in a distinctive house disappear into the larger composition of roof and wall shapes, siding and trim.

same windows in a larger house would look too small, perhaps, and the scale would be off.

The type and size of the windows should also be consistent with the exterior siding and trim. If your house has horizontal clapboards, then it's likely that your window and door types and the pattern of the window panes would reinforce that horizontal look. That's why it's silly to see a New England colonial with a picture window in place of the original multipaned, double-hung windows. If the view out the picture window is that important, there are ways to accommodate it without sacrificing the exterior harmony. (One way to do it would be to make sure the glass of the larger window had the same proportions as the smaller panes of glass in the windows in the rest of the house.) A distinctive house will have windows that almost disappear—you don't notice them individually but rather as part of an overall pleasing composition.

A wall of sliding doors and screens practically puts this master bedroom outdoors. This room (obviously) faces a private yard, while the high windows on the rear wall screen the room from the neighbors and help cut down on glare.

Windows are typically placed one over the other, but they don't have to be. In this house, the windows are stepped to reflect the placement of the stair inside. The unusual arrangement is balanced by the shed-roof window and its canopied counterpart below.

WINDOW RULES

There are three rules of thumb for positioning windows to help make a house distinctive. Following these rules will help you achieve a window mix that is unique to your own house.

- Place windows to take advantage of the outside views of the site, sunlight, and ventilation.

- Size and position windows in a way that corresponds to the positioning and importance of rooms in the plan.

- Make sure the windows have a pleasing visual composition that balances with the amount of wall and its siding, trim, and texture.

The more expansive wraparound windows of the living area wing of this house are a nice contrast to the solidness of the chimney and the two-story bedroom wing with smaller windows.

Stone has strong texture and pattern, especially when the stone and mortar are both left rough. On this gable end, the stones are larger every five courses, adding yet another level of variation.

TEXTURE AND PATTERN

Texture and pattern are two other features that are important up close. Again, variety and harmony are the key factors here. Combining different materials—rough and smooth siding, for example, or stone, stucco, and wood—can enliven the exterior of any house.

Exterior materials are like fabrics. They can produce a touch of elegance or a rustic quality, playfully highlight a fun pattern or establish a rigid order. The choice of siding, for example, can give a house a variety of qualities—horizontal or vertical, rustic or refined. Flat boards placed vertically with joints every 6 in. give a house a strong vertical look. The same house with horizontal clapboards would not look nearly as tall. Using wide-exposure clap-

MIX AND MATCH

Most exterior siding comes in two textures. One side is rough, the other smooth. You might decide to use the rough side facing out on the lower half of your house and the smooth side in on the upper half. Just that small change in texture will make a difference in how the light plays off the siding. It will also make a difference in how the siding looks when painted or stained.

Texture can also be the result of the siding choice you make. Shingles, for instance, have a very different texture than flat boards and stucco. Mixing and matching these texture choices can add a great deal of variety to the exterior of your house.

In this New England house, the variety of materials gives a playful but highly livable quality.

Variety in pattern, texture, and color can be combined to produce limitless siding options. Here, horizontal clapboards surround the lower level of the house just above the fieldstone skirt. Gables are board-and-batten vertical siding, and a band of herringbone decoration in between wraps the entire house.

The patterns and textures of the base, middle section, and roof of this building are distinctly emphasized by playing natural-finished shingles against painted trim. The base flares at the bottom, firmly planting itself on the stone terrace that connects the house to the site.

boards for the first floor of a house with narrow spacing on the second floor adds variety, but it also lightens the load of the second floor, possibly reducing the scale or mass of the building. Mixing clapboards with shingles, rough siding and smooth, or using horizontal siding with vertical board-and-batten siding have similar effects. This kind of variety can really transform an exterior, elevating it above the monotony of a house sided with the same material and spacing everywhere.

THE ART OF SIMPLE SIDING

*I*t doesn't take much variety in texture and pattern to transform an exterior wall. In this New England house, the exterior is made up of just two materials: cedar shingles and vertical board siding. But a closer look reveals that the shingles are more tightly spaced at the lower portion of the wall (starting at the door) and have a decorative pattern at the peak of the roof. Those two variations alone give the wall a more interesting texture and help differentiate between the roof and lower portion of the house.

The vertical siding, separated from the shingles by a continuous horizontal trim board, highlights the difference in texture by emphasizing the roof portion of the house even more. Roof and vertical siding are expressed as one unit, separate from the wall below. The combination and pattern of the siding gives the house a clear and even traditional form. Like a column, it has a base, a middle, and a top that is much more appealing than one monolithic color, texture, or pattern throughout. The resulting scale and massing are appropriate to such a small cottage-like house.

A variety of textures and patterns can be achieved with even a simple palette of materials. Here, vertical wood boards and variously shaped wood shingles applied at different spacings add a great deal of visual interest.

The horizontal pattern of the walls of this house helps offset the strong slope and texture of the wood-shingled roof. The pattern is created with natural-finished horizontal boards separated by a deep groove that houses metal flashing.

Simple or complex, an elegant roof always carries with it a deep significance and meaning about the house that lies beneath it.

The Roof: A Hat for Home

If windows are the eyes of a house, the roof is its hat, protecting it from the weather and adding a bit of personality. At the same time, a roof is the strongest visual element of a house. Roofs seem to say something to us all about shelter, the fundamental purpose of a house. One of the reasons the New England Cape Codder is so appealing is because of its simple, uninterrupted roofline. But for me, the roofs of many late-nineteenth-century Victorian houses are just as appealing because of their seemingly infinite variety and complexity. Simple or complex, an elegant roof always carries with it a deep significance and meaning about the house that lies beneath it.

A distinctive roof has a personality that's strong but not overwhelming. Roofs are as much about practicality as they are about looks.

ROOF, SITE, AND PLAN

Other than practical considerations (shedding rain or snow), there are no rigid formulas for selecting a roof style or type. I start the process of roof design by trying to match the basic roofline with the qualities of the site itself.

If a house perches atop a low hill, for example, a sheltering, umbrella-like shape will look better than a flat roof, because it will act as the summit of the hill. (Remember Wright's dictum, and think *of* the hill, not *on* it.) A wooded site would call for something different, perhaps a roof made up of a variety of shapes that contrast with (or complement) the forest. Another site might suggest multiple dormers to capture light and views. Sometimes, a steeply pitched roof fits better in the neighborhood

A strong roof form steps its way down over the plan of this house, finally settling on the stone wall that connects it to the landscape. And note that a roof need not be symmetrical—the three square windows align vertically but are offset from the roof peak.

The continuity of this long, sheltering roof along the water's edge was an important design consideration. Rather than break it up with a gable or dormer, part of the eaves was peeled back to create better views (and more natural light) in the second-floor bedrooms.

Roof, Site, and Plan Work Together

This small house sits on an expanse of abandoned agricultural land, overlooking a pond in northwest Vermont. From a distance, its simple massing and hatlike roof give the house a distinctive look, but what's most remarkable is the way the roofs, plan, and site are intimately connected.

Entry to the house is on the flat, somewhat opaque north side under a one-story appendage that is sheltered by a narrow shed roof. Inside, you immediately step into the main interior space, which is covered by a long, gently descending shed roof. This main living space is also defined by a curved wall of windows that unfurls like a sail as the space swells out in direct response to the site, providing south sun and expansive views. The long shed roof sweeps out over the east- and south-facing deck, offering protection like the brim of a hat. A two-story tower at the west end of the house, containing bedrooms and baths, rises up under a gable roof. Each roof defines a particular function and is related in turn to the plan needs and the site.

From afar, the simple elegance of the rooflines defines the various elements of the house: entry, living, porch, and bedrooms.

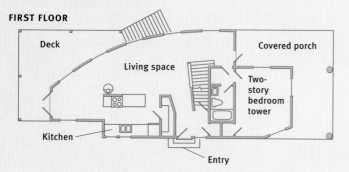

FIRST FLOOR

Deck

Living space

Covered porch

Two-story bedroom tower

Kitchen

Entry

This condensed plan sweeps out along a curved wall of many windows in direct response to the site.

The transparent south elevation of the house contains most of the windows and doors, providing good sun and views. The solid of the wall and the voids of the windows, at various heights, establish a harmonious rhythm both inside and out.

The long, descending shed roof over the main living spaces acts like a hat's brim, providing shelter from the weather.

A simple roof and plain exterior details are the perfect exterior expression of a simple, compact, and open floor plan.

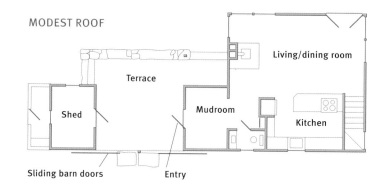

with other similar houses, while also giving the occupants more room underneath.

It's important to consider the floor plan, too. The roof over a small cottage would likely be simpler and more compact if the floor plan within had only a few rooms. A more traditional floor plan with lots of rooms (a comprehensive plan, as described in the previous chapter) would benefit from a roof with more variety, mirroring the layout of rooms beneath it.

MAIN ROOF, MINOR ROOFS

As a floor plan becomes more complex, it's likely that the roof will become more intricate and require minor roofs that complement the main roof. While many different roof types might work, the

MULTIFORM ROOF

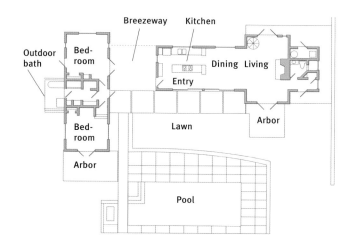

When there is more going on inside—more rooms, each with different functions—the complexity within is usually expressed by a more complex and varied roofline.

design needs to establish a clear visual pattern that differentiates the main roof (or roofs) from smaller, subordinate roofs. Harmony needs a major and consistent theme. Without a theme, the roof could look like a jumble of parts.

The main roof usually has the highest ridge (the top point of the roof), and it's the dominant shape around which all the other minor roofs flow. It sets the theme, and the minor roofs become variations on that theme, so it should be clear which is the main roof. This doesn't mean that the main roof is only one shape. It can be made up of many gables, hipped, or flat. Whatever it is, it should be the dominant shape.

Roofs with a clear visual order look less busy; they seem to fit better. That's not to say that roofs can't be complex. Some of the most interesting are staggering in their variety; but even in their complexity, these roofs transmit an underlying order, a delicate

A complex roof with lots of gables, dormers, and a variety of slopes and shapes needs to have a clearly identified major roof—usually the largest roof section with the highest peak—to establish a sense of order.

ROOF PITCH

The pitch of a roof is the angle it takes in relation to a horizontal line or, in other words, the floor plane. All roofs have some pitch—even flat roofs—because water needs to drain. What is the most appropriate roof pitch? There's no formula. Roof pitch should be a balance between practicality and aesthetics, between designing a roof to drain water and matching it to the site, the floor plan, and other details of the house.

There are some obvious practical issues. Steep roofs shed snow, ice, and rain better than shallow-pitched roofs. Sometimes the material used to cover the roof—asphalt, metal, tile, slate, or wood—needs a minimum pitch to work most effectively. Equally important, steep roofs increase usable floor space without the need to build another full story of wall.

Asphalt- or, more accurately, asphalt/fiberglass-reinforced roofing can effectively shed the elements at

extremely low pitches, which means that roofs can be shallower in pitch, and roof rafters can be shorter, saving on materials and cost. This can be an advantage, but too often homes are built with the shallowest pitch possible simply because it is cheaper, with no consideration of how it might look. (This is one of the reasons many houses built since World War II have such shallow roofs.) Recently, there has been a return to steeper pitches on many suburban homes, but often for reasons of nostalgia rather than because they make the most sense. These roofs often seem to be a hybrid of roof types and pitches with no apparent order or logic. They lack the balance of a thoughtful roof that considers the site, the floor plan, the climate, the neighborhood, the contrast between major and minor roofs, and pitch, all of which can be combined to make a distinctive hat for the house.

Matching roof pitch whenever possible will integrate minor roofs with the major roof.

Porches and decks can do
more to add human scale and
distinctiveness to a house than
any other exterior element.

balance of shapes, sizes, and slopes. A strong main roof, no matter
how much variety is introduced later, can pull all the elements of a
house together.

Defining Details

Walls and roof are key elements of a distinctive exterior, but the
process doesn't stop there. Just as a good sentence contains more
than nouns and verbs, a strong exterior contains the same defining
details that add richness and interest. There are many ways to add

personality to a home's exterior (several of which I'll discuss in the next chapter), but none has the impact of entries, chimneys, and porches. These elements contribute to scale, massing, and proportion. If you stand up against an entry porch on a two-story house, you're not inclined to feel out of place. However, if you stand up against a door to the same two-story house without an entry porch, you'd more than likely feel overwhelmed by the scale of the high wall. This sense of scale is important to our comfort and one of the reasons that porches and other details add richness and interest.

ENTRIES

Many new houses are built with massive, formal front doors, which is odd considering how seldom these entries are used. For example, just down the street from where I live, a huge new house was built with colossal front doors under a two-story overhang supported by gigantic columns. But guess what? No one ever uses that door; everyone comes and goes through the garage. This is a sign that the entry has not been properly planned or integrated into the site or the plan.

For better or worse, most of us arrive home by car. So it makes sense to make the arrival from the garage to the house as pleasant

SCALE IN THE DETAILS
Adding an entry porch to a two-story house gives it a scale more appropriate and comfortable to our bodies.

A good entry is more about comfort and welcome than it is about show. It should be graceful and inviting, providing a taste of the house without giving it all away. The best entries create a kind of suspense about what's to come.

This pergola, which casts interesting shadows on the wall of the house at different times of day, creates an appealing path from the garage to the informal entry.

Two chimneys make a strong statement about the entry point to this house and act as visual bookends to its two distinct living pavilions.

as possible. Why wouldn't you want to be introduced to the best things about your house on a daily basis, much the same way a stranger would? It makes more sense to spend your construction budget on this frequently used entry than on an impressive but forbidding front door. The problem lies in thinking about entries as having two completely separate natures: one for show and the other for function.

A good entry isn't about show. It should have a graceful quality, be inviting, and be well proportioned to human scale. It should also feel as if it were part of the site and the house, not separate from them. If it's right, it will say "enter here" and nothing else. A good entry should also be about usage. A functional entrance is one that protects you from rain or snow while you wait and allows you to experience the best parts of your house in a logical sequence, whether you arrive through a formal front door or through the garage.

Aesthetics play a role as well. Formal or informal, the threshold of a house ought to be welcoming, whether you live there or just happen to be visiting. Great natural light, a place to sit and take off your boots, and room for more than one person to climb into their coats are essential.

CHIMNEYS

Not all houses have or need dramatic chimneys, but I try to include one in all my designs. Nothing quite transmits a timeless sense of warmth, comfort, and solidity as much as a chimney. I often think of them as stakes in the ground around which the house rotates. There's something magical about a tall chimney against the background of varied roof shapes. To emphasize this vertical, steeple-like element, I sometimes even extend the chimney higher than required by code (typically 2 ft. above the nearest part of the house roof within 10 ft.).

Nothing quite transmits a timeless sense of warmth, comfort, and solidity as much as a chimney.

A chimney transmits timelessness—suggesting warmth, shelter, and comfort—and provides an opportunity to anchor a house to its site by its shape, color, and materials.

Chimney caps (in this case copper) keep leaves out of the flue and are light enough in appearance to counter the mass of the chimney below.

Building a good chimney can add to the cost of a house, but it can be one of its most distinctive features. As with all good details, it's the nature of the material that sets the tone for the resulting image. If I'm choosing between brick or stuccoed block, I make my choice on the basis of other influences or materials in the house, both exterior and interior. I might choose to use stone (usually more expensive than brick or block) because there's already stone on the site. I sometimes use stucco to match the base of the house, creating a combination that anchors the house to the site. Whatever the choice, the chimney never stands alone.

Chimney tops are another important ingredient. We often use chimney pots—somewhat simple when the chimney is stucco and a bit more ornate when the chimney is brick. Or instead of a pot, we might set off the chimney top with a cap. Caps are typically made of copper, stone, or concrete. Over the years, I've found that pouring a concrete cap in place seems to work best. (Lifting a piece of concrete or stone requires a crane.) Whether you use a pot or cap, either one will help define your chimney better against the sky and set your house off from a distance and up close.

A ZIPPER CHIMNEY

The power of a chimney comes from its materials more than anything else. This might mean using the dimension of the stone or brick to provide texture or reveals on the face of the chimney. Or it could mean something as simple as changing the color and patterning of brick. Chimneys can make a strong visual statement if you use contrasting materials, like this zipper pattern, created by adding white bricks against red. Here, this detail not only increases the vertical perception of the chimney but also sets it off against the green roof with its own white stripe. This is not an expensive detail; all that is required is a cooperative mason who is willing to work with two colors of brick.

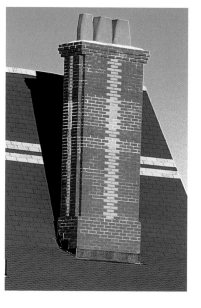

A simple zipper stripe made up of a different colors of brick can give a chimney a distinctive look. Here, it complements a stripe along the roof, formed by alternating courses of contrasting shingles.

Porches provide shelter **from the elements and, just as important, they open up interesting opportunities to create alternative spaces away from the main house. Because they are outside, they tend to be less formal and often more rustic and natural.**

PORCHES AND DECKS

Porches and decks can do more to add human scale and distinctiveness to a house than any other exterior element. Outdoor spaces like these are where we tend to let down our guard. They belong to the house, but they are also a special world apart. Both public and private, they can be formal or informal. They protect us from the elements but allow us to enjoy the outdoors in an almost vicarious way.

Even though they can be used for sitting, dining, sleeping, or just relaxing, porches and decks act as a kind of relief valve from the daily activities of the rest of the house because of their (usually) informal quality. It's that aspect that makes them fun to design—they always offer an opportunity to push the limits with unusual or whimsical details. It's also a chance to be just a little frivolous or to add some quirk, a bit like using an upturned collar on a shirt or fringe on a dress.

Like all elements of a distinctive house, a good porch or deck should always be integrated into the rest of the house and never just tacked on. Because these spaces actually connect and share

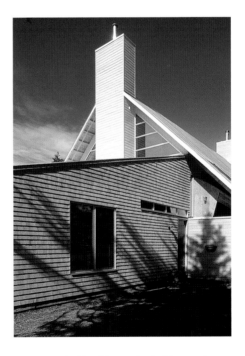

Even though this chimney is clad in wood, **its visual sense is perfectly consistent with the other expressed structural elements of the house.**

both the interior and the exterior, they present a wonderful opportunity to respond to the site and the floor plan. One way to tie a deck or porch into the floor plan is to extend an element from indoors, such as flooring or ceiling materials, or to use a rail detail both on an exterior porch and on a staircase inside.

Porches and decks come in all shapes, sizes, and purposes. You can adjust their shape to accommodate a slope or to make way for a chunk of ledge. A porch can lie under the main roof of the house or extend off the main house like a saddlebag. It might be fully or partially covered, making it part porch, part deck. Some of the most effective porches and decks are those that are a little of both, almost as if they had grown out of the house.

As we've seen in this chapter, general considerations such as scale, mass, and color, as well as specifics such as walls, windows, and roofs, all play a role in balancing exterior function and beauty. In the next chapter we will determine how certain details can enhance and even further this harmony.

Porches can be open or sheltered, small enough for just two people or spacious enough for a big party. Wherever they are, they should feel integrated with the rest of the house and never just tacked on.

A House of the Woods

WHEN I FIRST SAW THIS HOUSE, I was reminded of the wooden tent platforms I used to see in the parks my family camped in when I was a child. And as it turned out, I wasn't that far off. The house sits on the site of a cabin that had been in the family for years. The woman of the couple who lives there now had spent a lot of time at the cabin in her childhood, so when she was ready to settle down as an adult, she decided to build her permanent home on the site of that old cabin, which occupied a clearing overlooking Washington's Sequim Bay.

This is a house that belongs in the woods. Not only does it rise up out of the floor of the woods on a stone platform but its materials and colors, inside and out, connect it to the forest. The stone and heavy timbers make it seem as if it grew out of the landscape. It's more than just in the woods, it's *of* the woods.

An Ancient Ruin in the Woods

Before siting the house, the architect conducted an exhaustive survey of the property. He walked every square foot of the land and paid close attention to the smallest details. The survey included precise topographical information as well as the location of every tree in the potential building area.

That attention to detail paid off. The placement of the house seems natural, as

Rising up out of the forest floor, the house has the quality of an ancient stone ruin. The continuous foundation, chimneys, and stepped retaining walls around the entire house—all made from the same stone—serve to amplify the effect.

floor-to-ceiling glass, framing tree house–like views.

The exterior of the guest wing is more opaque. With the exception of the guest bedrooms and recreation room at one end, most of the space is more functional and includes the garage. The guest wing is more private, but it's a good complement to the more transparent main wing. In a harsher climate, such as the northeast, a more solid exterior elevation might be more fitting throughout the house. But in this temperate climate, the play between the opaqueness of the guest wing and the transparency of the living wing is one of the things that makes this house stirring.

The same stone used on the exterior appears on the fireplace in the living room. To emphasize the fireplace as a freestanding element, the architect inserted a small panel of glass on both sides of the fireplace between the stone and the wood framing.

The refinement of the interior is reflected in the warm honey tones of the exposed framing and natural cabinets.

Bringing the Outside In

One of the most appealing aspects of the house is the way its details and materials reflect the site. This is a house in which every stone and board says "Pacific Northwest." The basalt base wraps the house as if it rose up out of the ground to meet it. Inside, the warm wood tones of the floors, beams, ceilings, and cabinets—set off by stark white walls—echo the forest. It's almost as if the wood used throughout were actually cut from the surrounding forest. But this is no rustic cabin. Each interior material and detail is handled with a refinement that sets it apart from the ordinary.

Many details are shared between inside and out, blurring the lines between interior and forest. Timbers, for instance, protrude from the inside and come to rest on the stone retaining walls that lead down to the water. The exposed studs have a similar impact. They rise up to the ceiling in the master bedroom and form a low wall to place the bed against and an enclosure for the tub. The space left open above allows natural light to penetrate deep into the room while not shutting off the enclosed quality of the continuous roof. The low wall just above the tub is particularly appealing because it is made of translucent glass with just a few clear squares for selected views to the woods. Like all distinctive houses, these are details that belong intimately to both the site and the floor plan, producing a result greater than the sum of its parts.

Passing beams through the exterior wall and resting them on the stepped stone foundation creates continuity between inside and out.

One of the most appealing aspects of the house is the way its details and materials reflect the site.

In the second-floor master bedroom, the interior studs are left exposed above privacy screens of plaster or translucent glass, giving the whole room a floating and light-filled quality.

SECOND FLOOR

The master bedroom, with its tentlike roof, appears to float over the center of the living wing of the house, which is almost completely separated from the guest/garage wing (with recreation room above).

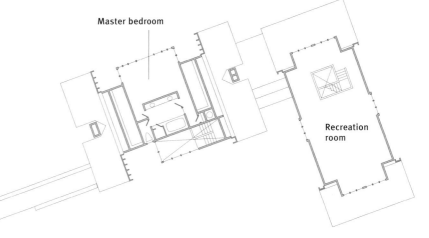

Master bedroom

Recreation room

The intimate realm

T he Finnish architect Eero Saarinen once said that the
solution to every design problem lies in the next highest
order. The best way to design a chair, for example, is
to think about the person who will be sitting in it. The same goes
for a home's many details. What's the best choice for a door han-
dle? Look at the door itself. How should the fireplace look?
Consider the room in which it will be the centerpiece. In a sense,
the best way to think about details is not to think about them at
all. Instead, look at them first in relation to the whole house.

This is a useful line of thinking when it comes to details,
because there are so many choices, and there's no surefire way to
know where and how to spend your time and money. Moldings,
staircases, exterior trim, doors, built-ins—these become the essence
of a home, the elements that make people say a house has character. But what's the best solution? Sometimes it's hard to know.

A well-detailed roof edge, like these exposed and stepped rafters, is an early indicator of quality and distinctiveness and one that can draw you into the intimate realm of the interior.

Details tend to work best when they are designed so that the natural qualities of the material are revealed in some way.

Details that are seen and used often, such as stairs, are opportunities to create a daily sense of attachment and an intimacy with the home's materials. Details also transmit a lasting impression of quality.

Considering all these possible details in the context of the next highest order will ensure, at least, that they'll relate to everything else about the house. The smallest detail—a custom-built front door, an unusual material used for a stair railing—can tie a home to its site. Sometimes a detail can literally share genetic material with some other element of the site (kitchen cabinets built from a tree on the property, for instance) or share history (such as a fireplace made of stone quarried from a place nearby). Other times, the connection is more subtle but equally powerful.

This chapter is about ways of *thinking* about house details rather than about the details themselves. Instead of agonizing about a particular detail, take a few steps backward—to the floor plan, to the exterior, and to the site. The big decisions have been made. What's left? What's missing? What doesn't belong? Some

details may simply reveal themselves. Others will require more work and difficult choices. The important thing to remember is that, as much as possible, the same considerations that went into the big decisions about siting and floor plans ought to be distilled in every detail.

The Power of Materials

Each detail is fashioned out of some material, and the stronger the connection between the material and the role of the particular detail, the more powerful the result. Think how strongly a wrought-iron latch and hinges on a front door transmit a sense of solidity and craftsmanship. The wrought iron could be rough and unadorned or delicate and refined, depending on the next highest order—the door, the trim, all the way up to the site itself.

Details tend to work best when they are designed so that the natural qualities of the material are revealed in some way. Wood can be smooth or rough-sawn, depending on the nature of the house. But having made a decision, say for rough-sawn clapboards, it doesn't make sense to paint them and hide the texture. Staining the siding or leaving it natural would allow the character of the material to show. This is not to say that all smooth surfaces should be painted or that rough surfaces can't be. What I'm suggesting is that details are most powerful when the materials themselves are used in such a way that their natural features and characteristics are highlighted, not concealed.

WHAT'S SO BAD ABOUT ALUMINUM OR VINYL SIDING?

It's always better to highlight the natural features of a material rather than try to conceal them. This is true for all materials—cost efficient, expensive, traditional, or contemporary. Take aluminum or vinyl siding, for instance. These are durable materials with great weather-resistant qualities. They can be manufactured in large sheets, they can be joined in a variety of ways, and they don't need to be painted. Unfortunately, most of the aluminum or vinyl siding you see is made to look like wood (and of course it never does). Why undermine the strength of this material by hiding it behind something false?

I have nothing against aluminum or vinyl. In fact, I've always wanted to design a house with this kind of siding; but if I did, I would make its finish look like aluminum or vinyl siding and not wood clapboard. I would let its unique qualities show. Whatever material you use, let the finish show the inherent nature of the material and don't use it as a substitute for another material.

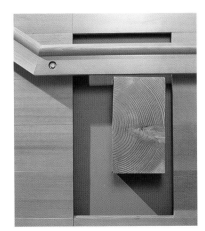

The materials you choose for details are as important as the details themselves. Here, the end grain of an exposed beam passing through a wall and into the stairway makes an interesting contrast to the stair rail.

The variety of texture and color between the rough stone chimney and wood-shingled roof, the smooth copper gutters, and the painted brackets and window casings is an interesting study in contrasts. What makes these details powerful are the materials themselves.

Details in Harmony

When you think about it, there really weren't that many materials to build a house from. Stone, brick, stucco, concrete, steel, and wood are the most common, though more exotic materials such as mud and straw are also possibilities. Whatever choice you make, a distinctive house is consistent in its use of materials, even at the most intimate level of detail. This house in the Catskills demonstrates a harmonious selection of materials in all its many details.

Details can be made up of many parts, and many details can be seen next to each other, and they should all feel as if they belong to each other. This level of attention to key details will give your house a pleasing uniformity by tying the various parts of the inside and outside together.

Consistency of materials results in a homogeneous look throughout. On the first floor, the floors, ceilings, trim, and built-ins—even the furniture—share the same wood tones. Details are also shared between interior and exterior, such as the steel joist hangers inside and the cross-bracing visible outside.

Though the walls on the second floor have a white stain, the natural look is similar to that of the first floor. Translucent windows on the stairway keep it private but bring in natural light.

Like a ribbon wrapping a package, trim adds a distinctive touch to the exterior.

Exterior trim can separate and unify **simultaneously. Here the white trim stands out from the natural stained siding and breaks up the first and second floors. But it also ties the various elements of the house together.**

Choosing the right materials is a key ingredient for successful detailing, but a home's details need to work together, too. If they don't, materials will compete with each other for attention. The best details not only stand out on their own but also unify disparate elements (or areas) of a house. One of the most useful tools for doing this is interior and exterior trim.

Trim is a catch-all term used to describe anything that is separate from the material used on the exterior body of the house (shingles or stucco, for instance) or on the interior (plaster or drywall). It includes moldings, baseboards, door and window casings, corner boards, water tables, rake boards, soffits, and fascia.

Exterior wall trim can help unify or separate various elements of the house. A wide horizontal trim board at the midpoint of a wall (called a *belt course*) can separate the first floor from the second. Using different siding materials above and below that trim board can push the separation even further. On the other hand, thin vertical battens applied over wider boards at equal spacing (called *board-and-batten siding*) can have a unifying effect.

Like a ribbon wrapping a package, trim adds a distinctive touch to the exterior. Not all houses need a lot of trim on the exterior, of course. Houses with little trim tend to emphasize the house as a whole (a unifying feature in itself), while houses with a lot of trim tend to emphasize its parts. Either will have a certain rhythm and continuity, which is the goal.

Similarly, interior trim also produces visual continuity between and among rooms and floors. Some interior trim, such as baseboard and window and door casings, is common in all houses. Other trim can be exclusive to a particular room, such as an elaborate coffered or beamed ceiling. I'll talk about built-ins later, but inside trim combined with built-ins can give any room a full-bodied quality. Baseboard tied to door, window, and ceiling trim that is, in turn, tied to bookcases will have an integrated look and feel that plain white walls won't have.

Trim can unify interiors **just as it does on the exterior. Here, a narrow piece of trim forms a continuous band around the room joining windows, doors, and fireplace. Matching the natural stain color of the trim with the floor, fireplace trim, window and door casings, and ceiling beams also helps unify the room.**

INTERIOR TRIM

Interior trim also has a practical purpose. It's a kind of cover that conceals junctures between the wall and ceiling and between a wood floor and a plaster wall. Trim helps conceal joints and prevent the likelihood of cracks caused by the joining of the different materials. Common baseboards and casings around windows and doors do just that. A number of architects in the twentieth century developed refined details that minimized or even seemingly eliminated the need for interior trim all together. This minimal look can be very beautiful when executed properly (see, for example, the top photo on p. 189), but the reality is that the labor required to install it can often be more expensive than using trim as a concealing detail. However minimal, interior trim defines edges, creates visual continuity, and can even protect walls from damage or wear.

In the houses I design, I often tie interior trim together by using a similar profile or portions of a similar profile on the baseboard and window and door casings. Tying just those two interior trim parts together in this way goes a long way to making a room feel unified. Both interior and exterior trim is expensive, so it makes sense to plan ahead and use material selectively. One-piece trim is the least expensive; trim made up of two, three, or more pieces—usually referred to as *built-up trim*—gets incrementally more expensive because it requires more material and labor.

EXTERIOR TRIM

Simple trim details using standard-size lumber can help enhance the continuity among the exterior elements of a house.

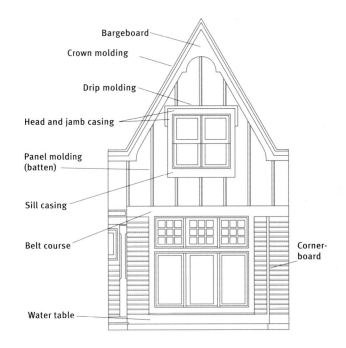

Bargeboard

Crown molding

Drip molding

Head and jamb casing

Panel molding (batten)

Sill casing

Belt course

Corner-board

Water table

INSIDE OUT

We tend to think of details as belonging either to the inside or the outside. Often they do, although some details are shared inside and out, with interesting results. A detail carried from the inside out (or the outside in) helps bridge the two domains, creating a more unified whole. For example, interior and exterior stair rails often have similar details. Exposed interior beams or ceiling lines can pass through the exterior wall and be revealed as rafter tails or a soffit on the exterior. This continuity lends an air of expansiveness—even to a small house— because the normal physical and visual barriers seem more transparent. Instead of having just four walls, the room includes the outdoors.

The exposed ceiling trusses inside this house appear to pass through the wall to the outside, where they form a trellis. Details like this break the barrier between indoors and out, making the outside seem closer and more accessible from indoors.

Defining Edges

For me, the areas between the ground and the wall and the wall and the roof are two of the most important exterior realms of a house. An elegant detail used at these points—at the start of the house wall just above the ground and at the roof edge at the top of the wall—can unify the exterior of a house in a unique way. This is where the body and roof of the house stop and start. It's at these two edges that the house physically and visually meets the ground on one end and the sky at the other.

The names typically given to these two edges are the *water table* and the roof *eaves* and *rake*. The water table is so called because it was originally a projecting molding or ledge at the bottom of a wall used to divert water as it fell from the roof and wall above. It's sort of a skirt along the bottom edge of the wall, separating the siding from the foundation. The eaves and rake are related details along a roof's edge. The eave is the lower edge of a roof parallel to the house wall, and the rake (sometimes called a barge board) is the sloped edge of the roof.

Houses don't need elaborate trim to be distinctive. In this elegant house with minimal trim, a recessed space at door-top height, which can be used as a picture hanger, pulls the room together.

The water table at the base and the roof eaves and rake trim help anchor a house to its site by uniting ground, wall, and roof.

Casing the Window

Casings—the trim that surrounds windows and doors—are important edge definers. Casings can unify wall openings with the rest of the design, making them stand out or blend in (see "Walls and Openings" on p. 145). A thick casing (1½ in. by 4 in. or larger) on either side of a wall tends to isolate a window or door in the wall—the opening seens more prominent. Narrow casing (or perhaps no casing at all) downplays the distinction between wall and window. You can also use trim to tie a number of windows or doors in a line together. This technique is sometimes called *picture framing,* because it gives the effect of framing all the windows or doors into one unit.

Sometimes no casing at all **can be appropriate. Here, the window frame itself butts up against the wall, drawing less attention to the window and therefore emphasizing the view.**

Casings are one of the only details on a house where inside and outside actually come together physically. If you open a window or door, you can touch both at the same time and see the thickness of the wall. This is important because casings help reinforce the character of the wall as a transparent or opaque barrier in much the same way that the size, pattern, or texture of the siding establishes the characteristics of the exterior wall. Yet casings are often the least considered detail of a house when it comes to thinking about inside and outside at the same time. All too often, they're seen merely as window or door surrounds; instead, like other distinctive details, they can help tie inside and outside together.

Picture framing a series of windows **by combining casings emphasizes the overall pattern rather than each individual window.**

Minimal casings **emphasize the windows and the wall structure as one continuous detail.**

A simple wood casing painted to match the wall can also put a greater emphasis on the geometry of the opening, the quality of the room, and the view. The window itself fades into the wall.

WATER-TABLE DETAIL

This water table is differentiated from the wall above by the use of a flat trim board with half-round trim applied to its bottom edge.

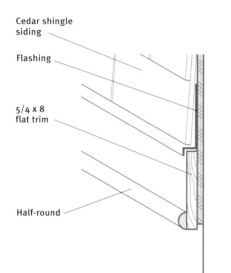

Cedar shingle siding

Flashing

5/4 x 8 flat trim

Half-round

A house can look radically different depending on the treatment of its base and roof. In these two houses by the same architect, the water tables and roof edges were not handled in the same ways, creating starkly different results. Yet each house fits its site perfectly.

It's surprising how much these simple and relatively inexpensive details can make or break a house, at least from a visual point of view. Let's take a look at two houses side-by-side. They have similar water tables but quite different eaves and rakes. The combination of edge details on both houses results in two very different looks. One house is compact, almost as if the wall and roof were one; the other emphasizes the difference between roof and wall.

The Connecticut house, shown at the top of the facing page, uses two flat boards painted a different color from the body of the house, emphasizing the water table, while the Massachusetts house, shown at bottom, uses the combination of one flat board and a half-round (so-called because it is a half circle) stained the same color as the body, de-emphasizing the water table. In both cases, the water table has a different texture than the wall shingles above, and that difference defines the beginning of the wall next to the ground. Without the water table, the juncture of wall and ground would seem coarse and abrupt.

The roof edges are also similar in one regard: they both have a thin knife-like edge that clearly differentiates roof from wall. But the amount the roof projects is quite different. The Connecticut house has hardly any overhang at all, whereas the Massachusetts house has a dramatic overhang made up of a sloping edge and deep soffit that completely wraps the building.

Both houses face south, and you might think that they would have the same long roof projections to block the summer sun. While this is a feature of the Massachusetts house, the Connecticut house takes a different approach, using the depth of the wall to help temper the sun at the living hall. The wall projects out beyond the face of the windows, acting as a kind of visor.

The areas between the ground and the wall and the wall and the roof are two of the most important exterior realms of a house.

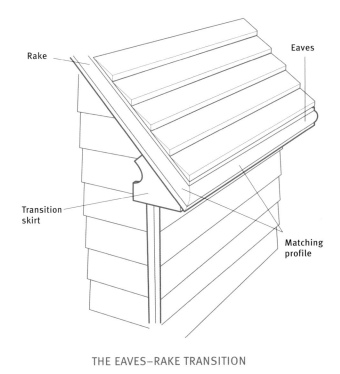

THE EAVES–RAKE TRANSITION

Using matching trim profiles and maintaining a similar pitch at the rafter tail and rake facilitates a smooth transition between eaves and rake.

Another interesting difference between these two houses is the meeting of the eaves and rake. This juncture is a good place to emphasize continuity. With the exception of the dormers, most of the roof in the Massachusetts house is made up of eaves only. The Connecticut house, however, has both rakes and eaves, and their meeting point is an important detail. It's at this spot that the continuity—or discontinuity—of the roof becomes apparent.

Different roof types or pitches can influence the way the rake and eaves meet. How the ends of the rafters are cut at the roof edge also can complicate matters. For instance, you might have a

The pattern of the exterior soffit battens, covering panel joints, continues through the screened porch wall and on to the interior ceiling. The continuity creates a subtle connection between inside and outside.

A soffit can affect the quality of light in a room. Here, the soffit, painted white like the interior, reflects light that bounces into the bedroom from the rocks and water below.

45-degree roof pitch, but the tips of your roof rafters might have a 30-degree pitch. This can make the juncture of eaves and rake difficult. One way to make this transition as smooth as possible is to use similar trim pieces on both the eaves and the rake and then to join them in a way that ensures as much continuity as possible.

SOFFITS

Another important ingredient of the roof edge is the soffit—the horizontal plane immediately under the eaves or rake. If the roof shape is revealed on the ceiling of the room inside, then the ability to see both the interior ceiling lines and the exterior roof edge at the same time is an effective way to carry the apparent interior sense of space and volume beyond to the outside. Ceilings or ceil-

The meeting of the eaves and rake is a good place to emphasize continuity.

A good entry door should not be about show. It should be functional, welcoming, and even a bit enticing, luring visitors to explore more about the house.

ing lines can be carried through the exterior wall and terminate on the exterior at the underside of the roof edge or soffit.

Soffits take many forms. They can be shallow or deep, smooth or punctuated with rafter tails or brackets. Another interesting aspect of soffits is their ability to reflect light inside. A deep roof overhang shades the sun, but a long soffit painted a bright color can reflect a lot of light into the house. One way to take advantage of this quality—and to increase the apparent transparency between inside and outside—is to paint or stain the exterior soffit the same color as the inside ceiling. If the color is light it will reflect more light into the room. In a bright climate you might even want to do the opposite: paint or stain both ceiling and soffit a darker color. This would reduce the amount of reflected light and glare.

Punctuation Marks

Certain details act like punctuation marks in a sentence. They can clarify parts of a house, join some parts together, even exclaim one portion over another. Exterior and interior trim act like commas, holding similar parts together. Other details, such as brackets, are like exclamation marks because they draw immediate attention. Your choice of what kind and where these exterior detail elements are placed can add another layer of interest and emphasis to your house. Some of the most useful ways to create these sorts of punctuation marks are through doors, brackets, columns, and rails.

DOORS

Literally and figuratively, exterior doors have more to do with the connection between inside and outside than any other detail. An entry door can be large or small, simple or complex in its components of texture; it can be all wood or all glass, painted or left natural. And like an entry, a good door should never be just about show or image. It should be about the rest of the house. All too often doors are an opportunity missed. In many new homes, doors are unique and exotic, but they bear no relation to the rest of the house in their material, color, pattern, or proportion. They stand out, but in the wrong way.

A well-designed exterior door, on the other hand, will impart a sense of transparency between inside and outside, inviting us to pass comfortably from one domain to the other. A door shouldn't call attention to itself but should provide a subtle invitation to the house. If you're intrigued by a house from a distance and then again close up, a good entry door should make you curious about the house's interior.

BRACKETS AND COLUMNS

Brackets and columns add emphasis to specific locations of a house. Unlike other exterior details, they generally serve a structural as well as a decorative role. Their size and shape can connote beauty and strength. The best brackets and

A solid door is effective at imparting a sense of durability, security, and privacy. A side glass panel allows the owners to see who's at the door.

A well-designed exterior door imparts a sense of transparency between inside and outside, inviting us to pass comfortably from one domain to the other.

Especially when they stand out in a contrasting color, brackets draw attention and can reduce the apparent scale of a house. They also help connect roof to wall by reinforcing a sense of structure.

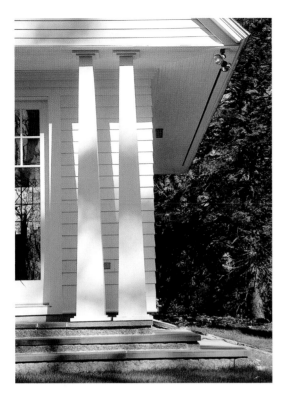

This simple, unadorned pair of columns sitting on a stone base support and augment the large roof overhang. The posts break up the wall, reducing the scale and mass.

columns designate both and seem to belong naturally to the house. For instance, a large wooden column or bracket would typically belong under a large or heavy-looking roof or overhang. There's obviously a delicate balance between what may seem too small, too heavy, or just right. You might also choose to use a contrasting material—such as steel—for the column or bracket, which may allow more options in terms of size. (Designed for use in the same place, a bracket made of steel would be smaller than one made of wood, expressing its natural quality.)

Rails

Whether lining a stair or ringing a deck, rails also have the quality of a punctuation mark. There are generally two types of rails, often used and seen together. One is a handrail, normally 30 in. to 38 in. off the floor or stair tread; the other is a guard rail with a minimum height (usually) of 36 in. As with other details, it's important to think of rails in relation to the house as a whole.

Rails can be one of the most difficult details to master. This is because the building code governs their size and configuration, setting some limits on design options. Since the 1980s, the allowable spacing between vertical or horizontal rails in residential work has decreased from 9 in. to 5 in. (to prevent small children from falling

Decorating Function

Bracing can have both a decorative and a structural purpose. The steel cross-bracing in this post-and-beam house helps stabilize three tall, slender columns on the exterior. The architect decided to let the function show through by clearly exposing the brace and the lag bolts that hold the brace plates to the columns. He carried the detail one step further by forming the plates into tree and owl shapes. This is a house in a wooded area, and that whimsical touch gives what could have been a nondescript detail an intimacy appropriate for the site and the house. It's a real punctuation mark.

Columns bunched together and stained impart a natural tree-like quality that is appropriate for this wooded site.

through the openings). This means that no matter what rail configuration you choose—vertical, horizontal, or otherwise—the spacing between those parts is somewhat predetermined. Because of the sheer amount of material required to satisfy code, it can be difficult to create a delicate and elegant wood rail. Sometimes a solid-wood rail can solve both problems at once; a steel rail, with more strength, may allow you to use smaller parts.

In recent years, I've tended to use metal components with just a touch of wood for my exterior rails. This is because metal rails require less maintenance but also allow me to make the lightest possible rail while still fulfilling safety and structural requirements. One of the most difficult aspects of rails is that they often block the view when you're sitting behind them. Cables solve this problem by minimizing the width of the material. From the inside they almost disappear.

Steel is typically more streamlined than wood. This combination of structural supports, balcony, rail, and trellis shows how steel parts tend to have a lower profile. Steel also is a nice complement to the stucco and glass.

Sometimes a solid-wood panel stair guard rail and a single wood handrail can be appropriate, especially when the floors, walls, and ceiling of the interior are also wood.

There are three interior details that can really make a difference: stairs, fireplaces, and built-ins.

An interesting combination of fireplace, bench, and loft stair create a strong room focus. Exposing the thin edge of the stone rather than the broad face reveals an interesting texture.

Window trim and stair details work together to give this staircase a monumental quality.

The Holy Trinity

A house is a balance of aesthetics, practicality, and affordability. Priorities must be set and choices must be made, but a few well-considered interior details can go a long way toward alleviating any compromises you might have to make. In my mind there are three interior details that can really make a difference—I like to call them *the holy trinity*: stairs, fireplaces, and built-ins.

Some interior details matter a lot to us because we live with them in a more intimate fashion than any other. They are more than just punctuation marks. We view the house only briefly from a distance, and see it close up once or twice a day, but you're likely to climb a stair, open and close built-ins, or even sit by a fireplace on more than one occasion during a day. For that reason, these components should matter to all of us. I built my first house for myself about 20 years ago. At the time, I could afford only a 1,200-sq.-ft. house, but I dedicated 10 percent of the total budget to cabinets, because I knew that I would use—and see—them more than anything else.

Some details are more affordable than others. Budgets are a reality, and the luxury of a well-designed fireplace or built-in can often be the first detail to be eliminated when the budget ax falls. But remember that all of our discussions throughout this book about details—inside and outside—have not been about the absolute necessity of any particular detail, but rather a way of thinking about what details you do use. It's not so important that you use any particular detail I've described, but rather that you relate what details you do choose to the site, plan, and exterior. A distinctive house has integrity because all of its parts are considered as one design element in a whole assemblage of components. No detail stands alone.

STAIRS

When I was growing up I lived in a two-story Midwestern four-square house that had an internal enclosed stairway connecting the floors; a door at the bottom entered into the kitchen. From a young age, I always wanted to take that door out and open the stair wall up to the kitchen. I was convinced that we should be able to see the kitchen as we came down the stairs, because the

A handrail set on undulating balusters and placed back from the edge of the tread creates the impression that this staircase is floating.

This small, compact staircase has a scale consistent with the rest of the house. The horizontal and vertical balusters align with the treads and risers, creating a graphic and geometrical effect.

Stepping Back in Time

Details are all about harmony. Usually this means that any one detail, like a staircase, would have complementary parts. The stair in this house seems to break that rule of thumb, but with good reason. It's a renovated stair made up of old and new parts. The old newel and balusters remain and are stained a dark color, probably as they were originally. The added handrail and horizontal guards, however, are made of new lightly stained wood. The contrast is strong and amplifies the difference between old and new.

But there's more to it than that. The horizontal guards on exposed vertical studs are certainly a contemporary treatment, but they also recall the old lath-and-plaster wall system that was part of the old house before it was renovated. In a way, the ghost of the old stair wall stands as a powerful reminder of what the old house used to be. It finds harmony in a unique and metaphorical way.

The new handrail is bolted to the exposed vertical studs, which also support the new lath guard. The spacing of the horizontal guards cleverly allows light through but separates the stairs from the areas around it.

Sometimes the brilliance of a detail is its ability to surprise or amuse. Here, the handrail is interrupted at the landing for a small sliding door that opens to the lower level.

This renovated staircase connects the new with the old by using two completely different handrail styles (one original to the house). The exposed horizontal lath recalls the plaster wall system of the original house. The choice of materials and colors amplifies the contrast.

Because the main stair in this house is in a public area near the front door, it has a higher quality of detailing than the private stair off the kitchen.

Stairs can take on great prominence as transitional spaces filled with expressive details.

kitchen was the one place where we all gathered each day. My mother and father had other thoughts; but it wasn't until I began to study architecture more closely that I realized that my initial intuitions were not so wrong, because the kitchen was quickly becoming one of the most important rooms in many American houses. Stairs can be exciting elements, a great connector between floors, and a wonderful part of a distinctive house.

You look at and use stairs in a different way than you do the other details. They may be an important design element in a space, but they are also an element you climb up and down and see from a variety of perspectives. This means that you need to think of them in a three-dimensional space, because you're likely to see all parts of the stair at different times. Stairs can take on great prominence as transitional spaces filled with expressive details. These details might include the way you design the tread or riser (the flat and vertical components of a stair), the kind of handrail or guardrail you choose, or perhaps the character of the space the stair sits in.

A small house on Martha's Vineyard has a good example of a stairway that plays a major role in defining the character of the house (see the bottom photo on p. 201). This is essentially a one-room house on two floors, and the stair design is integral to the overall character of the room in which it sits. Wood wainscoting is part of the stair walls, as it is with the rest of the house. The treads and handrails are natural cherry and match the cabinets in the kitchen. Even the stair balusters align with the treads and risers and seem to reflect the rhythms of the exposed ceiling framing above. This is what I mean by using a stairway to define the character of a space.

The size and character of the stair also have a lot to do with its placement in the plan. Sometimes the main stair between floors may be public, large, and somewhat ornamental because of its prominence in a major space; other times

it may be a private, small, and simple and used only by the family. Regardless of the size and budget of the house, any stair—large or small—is an opportunity to design something well. In fact, in a small house, it may be one of the best opportunities.

Fireplaces

Until the latter part of the nineteenth century, fireplaces in one form or another were an integral part of almost every room in a house. But as central heat became more prevalent—often in the form of a large coal-fired furnace in the basement—the use of the fireplace as a practical heating element went into decline. Today, with few exceptions, the fireplace has lost almost all its practical necessity. At best, it's only a secondary source of heat. Some furnaces and boilers no longer even need a chimney flue, eliminating any final vestige of association with the fireplace.

But for most of us, fireplaces still have great symbolic meaning, and they remain one of our most cherished details that we often

The surface texture of materials **adds depth to details. The thin, roughly cut edge of the stone of the fireplace surround is a nice contrast to the machine-cut flat face.**

Practical materials **can have interesting visual effects. Here, a masonry flue just above the hearth transitions into a metal flue, and the firebrick— normally reserved for inside the firebox—extends above the hearth.**

A Hearth Finds Its Home

The best way to imagine a fireplace—or any other interior detail—is to think of it in the context in which it sits. The fireplace of this house in Gloucester, Massachusetts, demonstrates how a design can be derived from the elements around it. The fireplace is one element of a larger interior landscape that includes a dramatic ceiling, an elegant staircase, and spare trim.

The stucco firebox and surround, carried above the mantle to the ceiling, reinforce the impression of the fireplace as an essential ingredient in the room. Stone from the site was used for the side wall and sitting area next to the fireplace, tying the interior design to the property itself. (It's almost as though the fireplace were part of the site and the house were built around it.) The view from the outside shows the same stone on the exterior and the same stucco of the hearth extending to the chimney.

This fireplace forges an intimate connection between the site and the house, one that is immediately noticeable to a visitor. The house is surrounded by rocky ledge; and once you enter the house, the staircase gradually steps down along the slope of the ledge to the massive fireplace. Some of the ledge was used in the sitting area next to the hearth, almost as if it were never moved from its original location.

RUMFORD FIREPLACES

*I*n my architecture practice I use only Rumford fireplaces, a fireplace design developed by Sir Benjamin Thompson, also known as Count Rumford, in the eighteenth century. To increase fireplace efficiency, he proposed a much larger but shallower opening. This meant that more heat was reflected back into the room, because of the increased wall surface of the firebox. To keep the fire from smoking, this design also meant larger flues and, therefore, larger chimneys.

For the most part, Count Rumford's theories and design guidelines were forgotten until the late twentieth century when there was a renewed interest in energy efficiency. Our firm began using them around 1980—but not just because of efficiency. It was also their size and relative scale in a room that intrigued us. A larger fireplace opening has more presence in a room and can be used as a more prominent design feature. We also try to match the material in the firebox and the exterior of the fireplace. A common mistake is to use a different color brick in the firebox or not to match the firebox material with the surrounding material. Different color bricks tend to detract from the overall harmony of the fireplace.

Because of their size, Rumford fireplaces, with their large openings, shallow fireboxes, and large chimneys, have a strong presence in a room.

The unadorned cabinets give this kitchen a compact, utilitarian quality.

One of the best
attributes of built-ins
is their ability to
tie together diverse
elements of a room.

Space is where you find it. A novel built-in bookcase along a staircase adds lots of shelf space and also makes this staircase warm and intimate.

include in our most important rooms. Fireplaces transmit a timeless sense of *hearth,* a figurative representation of the home itself.

BUILT-INS

One of the best attributes of built-ins is their ability to tie together diverse elements of a room. The best built-ins always feel essential to their room. We're all familiar with the most common built-ins: bathroom and kitchen cabinets. But built-ins can take many other forms, such as bookcases, benches, and audio-video equipment storage. The closer they are in size, style, and material with other interior details, the more likely they will feel integrated into the whole.

This is related to size, style, and material, but it also has to do with the basic designed order or rhythm of the room. The dimen-

Using the same wood on these dressing-room built-ins as on the floors, ceiling, and walls makes the cabinetry almost disappear into the woodwork.

Even a utilitarian laundry room can have a pleasing quality with built-in shelving.

sions of cabinet doors, shelves, and benches should make sense both within their own compositional order and within the overall dimensions of the room. For instance, along the length of any counter or wall, it is usually more pleasing visually to have built-ins of equal sizes or at least have a rhythm of sizes that are consistent. This might mean that all the cabinets are of equal size or that there is some attempt at matching the sizes.

There are no absolute rules governing such a composition. Beyond aesthetic considerations, practical needs play a role, too. It would be silly to design built-ins that didn't meet the specific size requirements of your books, plates, or other objects. But the thoughtful and pleasing composition of built-ins in a style and material that blends with the rest of your details can contribute greatly to a distinctive interior. This is why custom cabinets tend to feel more integrated than stock cabinets. But if custom built-ins are beyond the budget, you may want to consider painting stock built-ins with the same color used elsewhere on the interior trim. This imparts a kind of custom quality to the stock units, because they are coordinated with other details.

Distinctive Features

It would be a difficult task to write any book that included all the possible exterior and interior details of a house. Such a book would be more an architectural dictionary of details than one about design integration. I haven't attempted to include all such details but rather to show that some details may matter more than others and that, whatever details you decide to use, they should be integrated with all the other design elements of the house. Some details are distinctive by their very nature, simply because they are not as common as others. But like all good details thoughtfully considered, they can add another layer of interest.

EXPOSED TIMBERS

Exposed timbers or trusses fall into the category of special details. Timbers and trusses are exposed structural elements that support floors or ceilings. In most houses, structural members are concealed behind a layer of drywall, plaster, or wood, but they don't have to be. One of the big aesthetic advantages of exposing timbers as beams, rafters, or trusses is a more integrated look when combined with a wood finish at the ceiling or other areas of the room. This would also be true if the exposed structural members were made out of steel.

Another big advantage of exposing a home's structure is that the timbers establish a rhythm that can follow through to windows, doors, and columns or to other exposed structural members. This unifying rhythm integrates the space and ties diverse elements together (see the photo on p. 212).

Exposed wood structural members with finishes that match with other trim give a house a more integrated look.

The unusual combination of intricate wood trusses and a striped ceiling and chimney ties this room together, almost like the canopy of a tent.

TRELLISES AND PERGOLAS

Like timbers and trusses on the interior, trellises and pergolas on the exterior are another form of exposed structure, though they are often self-supporting and not essential to the integrity of the house. This means you can be a bit more playful when designing them. Generally speaking, trellises are vertical supports or frames used to attach a screen or latticework, and pergolas consist of vertical columns used to support a horizontal open roof of rafters. The delicate scale of each part of a trellis or pergola is one of the reasons they are so appealing. Breaking down the scale of the parts into smaller and smaller pieces is equivalent to adding siding trim or chimney caps to your exterior. In fact, one could say that all good details are composed of finer and finer refinement of parts. The closer you get, the more detail there is to see and enjoy.

Another appealing characteristic of trellises and pergolas is their potential to act as screens. You might want to block your view to the driveway or shield some of the sun from a sitting area. In each case, this screening quality adds a sense of transparency and expansiveness. The house shown on p. 214 is a good example. This combination of trellis and pergola sits in an open space created by carving away a portion of the roof mass to make a morning sitting

Trellises serve as partial screens and can help create transitional zones between inside and outside.

Some details are distinctive by their very nature, simply because they are not as common as others.

Two interlocking pergolas at an entry gate help define the intersection between the public and private areas of the house.

The combination of a vertical trellis and an overhead horizontal pergola provides a unique place to sit, with partial sun screening at a break in the roof.

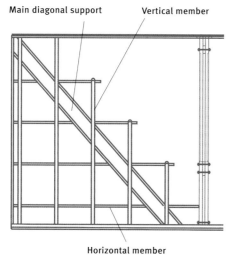

Main diagonal support   Vertical member

Horizontal member

DIMINISHING SCALE

The decreasing size and scale of the various parts of this trellis impart a sense of refinement, which any good detail should have.

area facing east and south. This is where you go on a beautiful day to watch the sun rise, have a cup of coffee, or read the paper. A little later in the day, when the sun is higher in the sky, you might also sit there under dappled sunlight if you didn't want the full shade of the covered porch around the corner.

THE NICHE

Most of the details I've discussed in this chapter have been actual building components, such as trim, rails, and exposed structure. But there's also another kind that falls somewhere between a room and a detail—the *niche*. This detail is actually a miniature space, quite small, with lots of elements that give it elegance and intimacy. Such a space is experienced as separate area within a house. Window seats, bays, cubbies, and nooks fall into this category.

I especially like these kinds of spaces, because you use them in such an intimate way. They seem to surround you. A combination window seat and cubbies in a house on Martha's Vineyard is just

By extending a roof just a small amount, you can gain enough room for a small sitting bay, as well as additional light and perhaps even a view.

such a niche space (see the photo on the facing page). This is a particular interesting example because it makes use of one of the most underused areas of any house: the space under a stair. Normally taken over by a closet or a half-bath, this design instead uses the space for sitting, reading, and viewing. The combination of finely detailed woodwork, cushions, bookcases, exterior window, light, and sloped ceiling gives this niche a feeling of warmth and intimacy that is very appealing. It also has a scale that's appropriate for adults and children alike.

Details should be part of our subconscious. We don't really think about them, but we enjoy them. Like the smell or taste of good food, they surround us and make the meal that much more satisfying. For a distinctive house, good details inside and out have that same quality. Without them, there's something about the house that seems flat or dull. With them, the experience of the house—first from a distance, then close up, and finally firsthand—is a fuller, more enjoyable encounter. In these times of uncaring design and often shoddy construction, pessimists want to tell us that the devil is in the details. But I would rather think, to paraphrase German architect Mies Van der Rohe, "God is in there, too."

Details should be part of our subconscious. We don't really think about them, but we enjoy them.

One of the most difficult spaces to use is underneath a stairway. This design makes good use of the space for an intimate sitting area, or niche.

Window seats make intimate and comfortable retreats, especially when they are oriented to capture sun and views and are part of a larger room.

Past as Present

WHEN I BEGAN STUDYING ARCHITECTURE, I got this valuable piece of advice: "Keep it simple, but make it complex." That's one of the reasons I've always enjoyed looking at houses from the past. Very often they have an outward simplicity and order that's enjoyable to look at, while underneath lies a complexity that comes only from thoughtful considerations of site, floor plan, exterior, and details. Old houses shouldn't be copied—that would result in a static, never-changing world of architecture. But they can be an inspiration and that is what's so intriguing about this Vermont house. It takes familiar elements, such as roof shapes and materials, and uses them in fresh and unusual ways, bringing them into the present. Architect Peter Rose says, "Architecture is such a dynamic process—there is no single instant when design happens." Likewise, there's no single instant when the past becomes the present. This house has elements of both.

Like a number of other rooms in this house, the living room resolves a common conflict between views to the north and sun to the south by opening to both sides. The space also steps down off the transparent entry to accommodate the gradually sloping topography outside.

The main house and a number of outbuildings set around an entry court give this compound the look and feel of a timeless, vernacular Vermont farm.

Big House, Little House, Back House, Barn

The house design began with the site itself. With the help of landscape architect Dan Kiley, the architect and owners settled on a spot where the slope gradually flattens. As with many of the houses in this book, visitors don't get a full view of the house at first. Instead, they pass through the woods and by a caretaker's house. It's a practical and subtle device, providing a sense of mystery and security to the arrival. Only after passing over a small bridge and then reaching an opening in the woods do you get your first view of the house, barn, shed, and garage sitting in a meadow.

This gradual arrival culminates in an entry court formed by the house and garage. Here, the distinctive wings of the floor plan embrace you by wrapping around the court and shielding it visually from the surrounding landscape. The placement of the equipment shed and garage also helps protect the paddock and entry court from the harsh winter winds

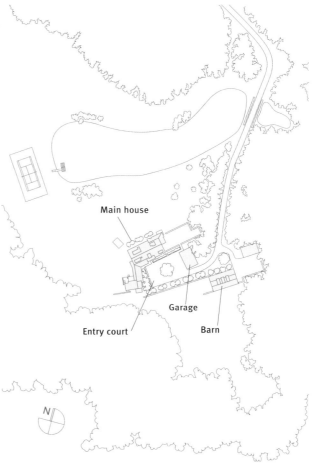

Main house

Garage

Barn

Entry court

N

SITE PLAN

The driveway winds through the woods, over a bridge, and past a meadow to arrive at the entry court. The journey helps define the relationship between house and site.

The slope of the main roof is reminiscent of an older Vermont farmhouse and is perfectly consistent with the gradual slope of the site and the vegetation around it.

Even though this is a complex house packed with many rooms, there's always a connection with the outdoors. Your position on the site is constantly referenced down corridors and through windows and doors to specific views of the outside.

that come out of the northeast. This plan is a contemporary interpretation of the nineteenth-century children's refrain from the book of the same name by Thomas Hubka: *Big House, Little House, Back House, Barn.*

Floor Plan Follows from Site

Like the succession of movements and buildings that define your arrival, the floor plan twists and turns to accommodate public or private spaces, views, sun, and ventilation. This is a traditional floor plan with a variety of rooms (rather than a more contemporary open plan). On the court side there are two entries—one formal and the other informal—while two independent studies are positioned to overlook the driveway and entry. Master bedroom, living room, dining room, kitchen, and guest bedroom all share the

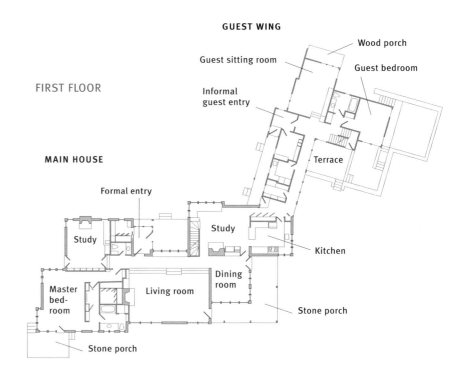

FIRST FLOOR

GUEST WING
Wood porch
Guest sitting room
Guest bedroom
Informal guest entry

MAIN HOUSE
Formal entry
Study
Study
Kitchen
Terrace
Master bed-room
Living room
Dining room
Stone porch
Stone porch

The simple, powerful roof is punctuated only where necessary by chimneys and simple shed dormers. The metal roof along with the concrete-block walls and mahogany windows blends with the colors in the landscape.

Throughout the house, custom built-ins were designed in materials of wood and stone that blend comfortably with the Vermont environment and help reinforce the connection to the site.

best views. A private sitting room for guests has a sunny exposure to the east, south, and west.

At first pass, the house seems to violate a cardinal rule in siting—windows should face south. Here the best views are to the north, although the best light is from the south. The architect resolved that conflict by making the floor plan only one room deep in places along its east–west axis. This means that many areas of the house are open and bright, even if they don't actually face south. In fact, each room gets direct sun—some, including the master bedroom and guest bedroom, get direct sunlight twice a day, depending on the season.

Simple at the Surface, Complex Below

Simple objects are sometimes beautiful because underneath their simplicity lies something incredibly complex. This is certainly true of this floor plan and roof. With its many rooms of various sizes and its circuitous circulation patterns, the plan is quite complex, yet it also has a simplicity that seems to be the natural result of the site and the homeowners' needs. This balance of simplicity and complexity is especially evident in its roof, where an uninterrupted shape—punctuated only by chimneys and dormers—has the same embracing quality as the floor plan.

This house is a good example of arriving at the exterior elevations, to some

extent, from the site and the floor plan. The roof is high only where necessary— over the two-story guest bedroom wing and the living room, for example. (A simple shed dormer through the main body of the roof boosts the natural light.) The roof is low only where it is less important, in areas such as transitional connectors or porches. Exposed rafter tails and the rhythm of the standing-seam roof add another layer of interest. Given its prominence, this could have been an overpowering roof, but it's not. It enhances the quality of a house that seems hunkered down to protect itself from the Vermont elements but also open in just the right spots for views and sun.

An elegant, single line of steel handrail connects the two floors of the guest wing with a private outside terrace.

The introduction of steel in various locations, whether at balcony rails or at a living room ceiling beam, is a statement of the need to blend contemporary structure with traditional spaces. Steel also complements, and even supports, the custom light fixtures.

Details That Are More Than Distinctive

The best architecture is different in some aspects—it's unusual or unexpected—but it also has to be good. The same is true for details. In this house, details that may seem unusual or different are also good details because they tie into other elements of the site, the floor plan, and the exterior. This house is filled with such details, yet none of them seems out of place.

Consider the use of concrete block on the exterior. According to architect Rose, "Anything that costs as much as architecture, is going to be around as long as it is, and has such a great influence in our lives should endure and age well." That statement might have led him to choose expensive materials. Instead, he chose a cheaper material but with a creative twist. By mixing reds and warm limestone into the cement mix he was able to produce

Distinctive houses are always a balance of past and present.

buff-colored concrete blocks with subtle variations of hue that blend with the wood trim and metal roof of the house, not to mention the natural colors of the New England landscape. By using this durable, inexpensive material in this way, he gave it qualities that are different.

The wood ceilings throughout the interior are another unexpected detail. This is not an unusual detail by itself. One might typically use wood at higher ceilings in large rooms. But here wood is also used for many of the lower ceilings in the entry and corridors, imparting a more intimate character than plaster or drywall would. In one room, the wood ceiling continues from a corridor to the underside of the balcony that overlooks the major living space. The effect is of a balcony with a much lighter, floating quality that doesn't overwhelm the living space below.

The roof is an ever-present part of experiencing the house. Its comforting quality is especially apparent at the porches off the ends of the house.

Steel is also used in interesting ways in selected parts of the interior (see the photos on pp. 224–225). One instance is the steel handrail at the guest stair, which seems to float like a fly-fishing line as is moves its way down the stairs. Likewise, a steel supporting beam at the peak of the living room ceiling, which is detailed predominately in wood plaster, is the simplest and most direct way to make this span. In a way, it's a metaphor for the whole house and similar to what a farmer might have done if he had built there 200 years earlier.

Distinctive houses are always a balance of past and present. They have a timeless quality that connects both by continuing the traditions we are familiar and comfortable with and, at the same time, enhancing the conditions of our lives today. This house in Vermont is a wonderful example of that continuity. But more than that, it's also an example of what we can all have if we pay close attention to the site, the floor plan, the exterior, and the key details inside and out. A truly distinctive house is not just about a collection of those design elements; it's also about the connection among them. When each is considered thoughtfully and the relationships are evident, the house will belong to all of us for all time.

ALBERT, RIGHTER & TITTMANN
ARCHITECTS, INC. (pp. 57, 145)
58 Winter St.
Boston, MA 02108
(617) 451-5740

STEPHEN BLATT ARCHITECTS
(pp. 70–71, 171)
10 Danforth St.
P.O. Box 583 DTS
Portland, ME 04112-0583
(207) 761-5911

BOHLIN CYWINSKI JACKSON (pp. 50,
84, 133, 159 top, 183 left, 202-203)
123 South Broad St., Suite 1370
Philadelphia, PA 19109
(215) 790-5900

TURNER BROOKS ARCHITECT
(pp. 160–61)
319 Peck St.
New Haven, CT 06511
(203) 772-3244

CASS CALDER SMITH
ARCHITECTURE, INC. (pp. 18 top left, top
right, 26, 27 left, 42–43, 82 bottom, 86
bottom, 94–95, 162 bottom, 190 top,
205 bottom, 213 bottom)
522 Second St.
San Francisco, CA 94107
(415) 546-6470

CATALANO ARCHITECTS (pp. 85 bottom,
106, 138, 143 top, 197 bottom)
374 Congress St.
Boston, MA 02210
(617) 338-7447

CENTERBROOK ARCHITECTS (pp. 18 bottom, 19, 36, 97 bottom, 108–109, 137,
156 top, 163 bottom, 166 right, 181, 190
middle, 197 top, 205 top, 212)
67 Main St.
P.O. Box 955
Centerbrook, CT 06409-0955
(860) 767-0175

ROSS CHAPIN ARCHITECTS (pp. 10 bottom, 11 bottom right, 82 top, 83 top,
112–13, 139 top, 165 left, 182 top, 186)
P.O. Box 230
Langley, WA 98260
(360) 221-2373

CUTLER/ANDERSON ARCHITECTS
(pp. 24, 40–41, 45 bottom, 88, 146 bottom, 172–79, 184–85, 198 bottom left,
bottom right)
135 Parfitt Way SW
Brainbridge Island, WA 98110
(206) 842-4710

JEREMIAH ECK ARCHITECTS (pp. 6, 8–9,
14 top, 16, 22 top, 23, 27 right, 29, 30,
32, 34–35, 38–39, 46–47, 53, 60–61,
63, 68–69, 72–79, 87, 92, 93, 99, 103,
104–105, 130, 131, 135, 136 top, 147, 156
bottom, 159 bottom, 163 top, 164, 165
right, 166 left, 168 top, bottom, 189
bottom, 192 top, bottom, 194–95, 198
top, 201 bottom, 204, 206–207, 208,
214, 217)
560 Harrison Ave.
Suite 403
Boston MA 02118
(617) 367-9696

ELLIOTT & ELLIOTT ARCHITECTURE
(cover, pp. 48–49, 98, 114–15, 143 bottom right, 144, 146 top, 150 top, 182
bottom, 191, 210 bottom)
Main St.
P.O. Box 318
Blue Hill, ME 04614
(207) 374-2566

ESTES/TWOMBLEY ARCHITECTS (pp. 10
top, 13, 22, 25, 28, 64–65, 86 top, 97
top, 132 right, 143 bottom left, 152 bottom, 153 bottom, 154 bottom, 162 top,
165 middle, 167, 183 right, 190 bottom,
196, 200 left, 201 top, 209 top, 211)
79 Thames St.
Newport, RI 02840
(401) 846-3336

FERNAU & HARTMAN ARCHITECTS
(pp. 17, 107, 110–11, 199 bottom, 216)
2512 9th St. #2
Berkeley, CA 94710
(510) 848-4480

PETER L. GLUCK & PARTNERS (pp. 51–52,
189 top)
646 West 131st St.
New York, NY 10027
(212) 690-4950

GRAHAM GUND ARCHITECTS (pp. 120–29)
47 Thorndike St.
Cambridge, MA 02141
(617) 250-6800

MARK HUTKER & ASSOCIATES
(pp. 116–17, 153 top, 188 209 bottom)
P.O. Box 2347
Vineyard Haven, MA 02568
(508) 693-3340

LAKE, FLATO ARCHITECTS, INC. (pp. 83
bottom, 89, 154 top)
311 3rd St. #200
San Antonio, TX 78205
(210) 227-3335

JONATHAN LEVI ARCHITECTS, INC.
(pp. 66, 157)
266 Beacon St.
Boston, MA 02116
(617) 437-9458

ROBERT LUCHETTI ASSOCIATES, INC.
(p. 56)
14 Arrow St.
Cambridge, MA 02141
(617) 492-6611

BRIAN MacKAY-LYONS ARCHITECTURE
(pp. 45 top, 118–19, 169 bottom)
2042 Maynard St.
Halifax, Nova Scotia
Canada
B3K3T2
(902) 429-6276

McINTURFF ARCHITECT (pp. 62, 132 left,
139 bottom, 148–49)
4220 Leeward Place
Bethesda, MD 20816
(301) 229-3705

JAMES McNEELY ARCHITECTS (p. 100)
66 Beacon St.
Boston, MA 02108
(617) 367-3655

MOUNT VERNON GROUP (p. 31)
20 Cabot Rd.
Woburn, MA 01801
(781) 937-9720

CHARLES ROSE ARCHITECTS (pp.
54–55, 170, 199 top)
115 Willow Ave.
Somerville, MA 02144
(617) 628-5033

THE OFFICE OF PETER ROSE (pp. 218–27)
1 Kendall Square, Building 1700
Cambridge, MA 02139
(617) 494-0202

SALA ARCHITECTS, INC. (p. 155)
43 Main St. SE, Suite 410
Minneapolis, MN 55414
(612) 379-3037

SHOPE RENO WARTON ASSOCIATES
(pp. 12, 136 bottom, 152 top, 200 right)
18 West Putnam Ave.
Greenwhich, CT 06830
(203) 869-7250

SCOTT SIMONS ARCHITECTS (pp. 80,
90–91, 169 top)
15 Franklin St. Art
Portland, ME 04101
(207) 772-4656

TURNBULL GRIFFIN & HAESLOOP
ARCHITECTS (pp. 58–59, 213 top, 215)
817 Bancroft Way
Berkeley, CA 94710
(510) 841-9000

VAN DAM & RENNER (pp. 7, 14 bottom,
15, 67, 140–41, 180, 210 top)
66 West St.
Portland, ME 04102
(207) 775-0443

DENNIS WEDLICK ARCHITECT (pp. 101,
102, 150 bottom, 151, 187)
85 Worth St., 4th floor
NY, NY 10013
(212) 625-3838

PHOTOGRAPHERS